THE "IDEAL" COURSE IN NEWS WRITING AND CORRESPONDENCE

By Julian J. Behr

FOREWORD

In preparing this course of lessons it is the aim of the author and editors to give to the student just those points necessary to start him on the right road to a career in Newspaperdom, and to give him (or her) those points in as brief and emphatic a manner as is possible.

Bear in mind as you commence your study that there is no finer career than that of the modern newspaper man or woman. As to opportunities--they are unlimited. More and more, newspaper work is being looked upon as a career in itself--a well-paid career by the way--but it also is a stepping stone to other fields of literature. Many of the famous authors--yes, most of them--started in newspaper work and many of them continue to devote a part of their time to the daily press.

There is room for hundreds of newspaper correspondents--there is a place waiting for you but you must make up your mind to stick--stick through thick and thin--for the newspaper writer faces one seemingly unsurmountable obstacle after another, and the overcoming of these is the glory of the task.

Adopt--now as your slogan--"It shall be done." Follow that unswervingly, and there is a success ahead of you far beyond your fondest dreams.

Lesson I.

NEWSPAPER CORRESPONDENCE A PROMISING FIELD.

Let it be understood right at the beginning that there is no pursuit more worthy, and none more promising than that of newspaper correspondence--which is the threshold of journalism. To those who possess a talent for the work and are willing to apply themselves and make the most of their ability, success is assured. Talent without industry will not win, although indefatigable energy and sheer love of the game have carried to a high position many a man whose natural talent for the work appeared to be nil.

The work of gathering news demands strict adherence to facts --a fair and open attitude of the mind that will not be swerved from the truth. Strenuous effort means nothing to your paper if your correspondence is colored and distorted by your own prejudices or preferences. News is fact--nothing more and nothing less; you must be accurate to survive in this field. Score one for correspondence as a builder of character!

It is no less a builder of incomes. Newspapers and press syndicates pay from $5.00 to $25.00 a column for acceptable news, depending on the ability of the writer and the human interest value of the news. You may earn only a few dollars a week at the start, either because of lack of material or your own unfamiliarity with news' values. But as you develop your "nose for news," your earnings will increase as fast as your knowledge. Even though you are located in a small town where few happenings of national interest occur, it is well to be on the alert for acceptable stories. The constant exercise of sight and hearing in your daily life will cultivate and

develop the habit of vigilance and is bound to be reflected in the character of your work as well as in the volume of news' items garnered.

Talent for a particular vocation is not always apparent. Often it does not manifest itself until one is fully aware of the requirements and begins to take genuine interest in the work in hand. In this regard, newspaper correspondence does not differ from any other line of endeavor. You may, as you read this, possess the talent requisite to make you a correspondent of the highest type; but you cannot be sure until you understand the nature of your work, and until you have discovered that you really love it.

Not infrequently a correspondent is called from an obscure town to take up larger duties in a city because of the native ability displayed through his work in a narrow sphere. More than one managing editor--more than one general manager of a big city daily--started his career as a local correspondent in a little town. It is well to remember that the eye of your editor is always on your work, even if he isn't directing it; applauding your progress with an approving nod or expressing his regret at your lack of it by the use of a merciless blue pencil.

In many instances correspondents have displayed decided ability in special branches, and when called to the staff of a metropolitan daily, are assigned to work for which they have shown great aptitude. This is where our famous sport writers come from; our theatrical critics--yes, and even many of our leading editorial writers. Men who are paid large fees for special articles on events of national interest, such as presidential elections, world series

baseball games, political conventions, etc., all begin newspaper life in humble capacities and earn their way by earnest, conscientious effort and unquenchable "love of the game." Your opportunity is greater because the field broadens and the rewards grow more attractive every year.

No one can follow the work of correspondent for the press for very long without being a better man. You meet people in every walk of life; you observe men and women in joy and in sorrow; you hear both sides of various controversies and lend a sympathetic ear to each. Every new experience has a broadening influence, makes you more tolerant of the shortcoming-- more cognizant of the virtues--of your fellowmen. In short, it makes you a better American citizen. The best proof of this statement lies in the editorial precepts of that sterling American, President Warren G. Harding, owner and publisher of the Marion (Ohio) Star.

The policies of this paper are of sound growth and are second nature to the staff. Managing Editor Van Fleet has been with the paper for thirty years and others have been there longer. They are thoroughly trained in Harding ways, and the creed of the Star needed not to be written out for them, and never was written until it was desired by others; then members of the staff reduced to words the Harding editorial precepts, as follows:

> "Remember there are two sides to every question. Get both. Be truthful. Get the facts. Mistakes are inevitable, but strive for accuracy. I would rather have one story exactly right than a hundred half-wrong.

"Be decent, be fair, be generous; never vindictive.

"Boost; don't knock. There's good in everybody. Bring out the good. Never needlessly hurt the feelings of anybody.

"In reporting political gatherings give the facts. Tell the story as it is; not as you would like to have it. Treat all parties alike. If there is any politics to be played we will handle it in our editorial columns.

"Treat all religious matters reverently. If it can possibly be avoided never bring ignominy to an innocent woman or child in telling of the misdeeds or misfortune of a relative.

"Don't wait to be asked, but do it without the asking.

"And above all, be clean. Never let a dirty word or a suggestive story get into type. I want this paper so conducted that it can go into any home without destroying the innocence of any child."

There, in a few words, is a creed that the prospective correspondent may well take to his heart and make his own. It sums up the ideals of American journalism. Study it. Believe it. When you do, you can't go wrong.

There are instances by the thousands of newspaper correspondents and reporters who have risen from obscurity to high position. The most striking example of the value of newspaper training was the presidential contest of 1920, when both the Republican and Democratic nominees were editors and publishers of newspapers. Both President Harding and Governor Cox had to earn their spurs in the hard

daily grind of news-gathering, and they climbed to the top through sheer merit and because they would not be denied.

Frank Vanderlip, the man who sponsored the United States War Savings Stamps, and formerly president of the National City Bank of New York, was for years a newspaper man. He is regarded as a high authority on banking throughout the United States.

Josephus Daniels, Secretary of the Navy in President Wilson's cabinets, was before the war and is now editor of a Raleigh, N. C., newspaper. United States Senator McCormick, of Illinois, owns the Chicago Tribune.

Charles Murphy, former owner of the Chicago "Cubs," covered many an assignment for newspapers in the Middle West, and President Ban Johnson of the American League, started his career as a reporter.

To go a step further, into the field of agricultural publications, we find that one of the candidates for the Republican presidential nomination at the Chicago convention, in 1920 was ex-Governor Arthur Capper, of Kansas, now United States Senator. Governor Capper wrote farm-news articles for the big farm papers long before he became a publisher.

It isn't difficult to understand the influence which their work had on these famous men, and their careers should be a source of inspiration to men and women who contemplate entering upon the work of news gathering. If you could visit these men and ask their counsel as to the best means for attaining success in your work, a summing up of their advice would undoubtedly approximate President Harding's creed as published in this lesson.

Two avenues are open to the prospective newspaper corre-

spondent. One has to do with the great press associations or syndicates, the Associated Press and United Press; the other with nearby county seat daily or weekly newspapers. Both of the big press associations maintain representatives in the big cities--but not in the small towns; while a city or small-town daily, or a county seat weekly welcomes news' stories from nearby communities, large or small.

If you reside in a big city, or wish to go to a big city to take up your work, write to the Associated Press or United Press in making application for a connection as a correspondent. On the other hand, if you prefer to remain in your home town and represent a nearby city newspaper, call on the editor of the paper.

Review Questions.

1. What is news? What is the first and most important quality demanded of the newswriter?
2. What creed should the correspondent follow?
3. What two avenues confront the prospective newspaper man?

Lesson II.

WHAT NEWS IS.

To write successful news stories, four requisites are necessary--a clear insight as to what constitutes a real news story; the stick-to-itiveness to get such stories; the ability to work rapidly, and the power to present facts accurately and interestingly.

Persons who are quick to recognize news value in events are said to have a "nose for news"--the first essential quality of the successful correspondent. It is obviously impossible to succeed if you do not recognize news when you see it. For example, if a man is bitten by a dog there is little if any news value in the event. But if a dog is bitten by a man, the very oddity of the incident would constitute a reason for its news value. News, in short, may be said to consist of an accurate citation of facts or ideas certain to interest a large number of people. The fault which proves the undoing of many correspondents is that they do not know a good story. You should, therefore, have a clear and definite understanding of what really constitutes news before you attempt to search for it, and before trying to write a news story.

The main consideration in a news story is accuracy. No newspaper wants to publish a story and then have to retract all or a part of it because the correspondent has garbled the facts. Besides, no newspaper will long tolerate a correspondent who is so careless.

What facts or ideas are certain to interest a large number of people? What constitutes interest in a story? Anything that provokes thought; that grips the attention of the reader, either by its abnormality, unexpectedness, closeness of the event, timeliness or

unusualness. Yet none of these is essential--not even timeliness. For example, if you learned today that a high-government official had killed a man in 1901, the announcement of the event would be news and every big-city daily in the country would carry it on the front page, notwithstanding the fact that the event occurred many years ago. Newness, things removed from the usual, and mystery, help make news, but they are by no means necessary. The fundamentals of news stories are facts or ideas which are certain to interest a great number of the paper's readers.

If you were correspondent for a county seat paper, it would be of more interest to the readers of your paper to learn that Tom Jones was buying a flivver than that the Secretary of State was purchasing six imported cars.

You will have to be ever on the alert for extremes, the boldest robbery--the largest pumpkin, the fastest motor car or trotter, the finest hunting dog, all of which are interesting news subjects. The newspaper reader loves extremes, and the "greatest" or the "least" of anything interests him. Events of an unusual kind, with queer twists of humor in them, make acceptable news items. For example: Burglar Steals a Rifle; Conscience-Stricken Tax Payer Sends in Money Held Out twenty Years Ago, etc. Human interest stories such as: "Boy Leaves School to Find the End of the Rainbow," are excellent happenings to chronicle. Contests are always interesting. Baseball or other sports; political rivalry, a struggle for supremacy between business men, society women; race horses or facts concerning rival cities is news material for the correspondent. The element of struggle for supremacy adds tang to any story. Stories of helplessness

that arouse pity and sympathy, known as "sob" stories among newspaper men, tell of "Blind Man Loses Life-Long Helpmate"--"Dog Saves Boy In Distress," mother's joy at her son's return after long absence, a child's suffering, are interesting to many readers. Dog stories that are well handled are always effective.

Prominent persons "make" news items. Anything no matter how insignificant, regarding a noted man, interests a great many readers. And even though the reader may never have heard of the prominent man, if his position is high, the reader is interested. Thus, the fact that the President shaves himself, or that the Prince of Wales smokes stogies, get attention. If Bill Smith, the corner grocer, got under his machine to make some repairs, the event wouldn't cause a ripple of interest. But if Chief Justice Wm. H. Taft crawled under his automobile to tinker with the mechanism, the news would create widespread interest.

Prominent localities, too, carry considerable weight with the newspaper-reading public. The very names of Atlantic City, Reno, Fifth Avenue, Monte Carlo--all summon up pictures with a meaning. Everyone likes to read of famous places just as they do of famous people. A fashion created in New York or Newport is read about and copied the nation over. An event of comparatively minor importance in the average town becomes interesting if it occurs in a nationally, or internationally famous, spot. A false alarm in the Vatican would excite more comment than a real fire in Oshkosh; or a conflagration in Pumpkin Corners.

New styles in women's or men's dress are good as news material. Novel creations in jewelry also furnish interesting reading

matter. A convention of tailors or dressmakers or haberdashers should be good for a column or more of news. If men's coats are to be a bit longer, their trousers roomier or their hosiery of more vivid shades and patterns; if ladies' skirts take pleats instead of ruffles, if their pumps are to be decorated with bows instead of buckles, and their hats are to be adorned with hay instead of feathers--all of this will be eagerly devoured by Mr. and Mrs. Newspaper Reader.

Any newspaper likes to print interviews with famous people on almost any subject. For example: Japanese Ambassador's Impression on American Sports; Head of Largest Bank Raises Airedales; Aviator Who Made Altitude Record Doesn't Consider Occupation Hazardous; Prima Donna of Paris Opera Says New Era of Music Is At Hand. The opinions of people "in the public eye" are read eagerly even when the subject itself is uninteresting.

Financial affairs which bear on the purse of the newspaper reader, make excellent news items. The information that the price of turkeys is to be prohibitive this Fall; that wage revision on railroads is expected to bring travel rates to a lower level, are messages of importance to newspaper readers. The outlook regarding prices on foodstuffs, clothing, etc., from authoritative sources, or the effect of a refunding bond issue on income taxes, gets ready attention. Keep in touch with grocers, market people, and business houses which receive market reports on foodstuffs. See them occasionally and inquire as to probable rise or fall of prices. Readers like to note any fluctuation which affects their pocketbooks.

It may be said then, in view of what has been outlined, that the only requirements of a happening or idea necessary to make it

good news material are that it be written accurately and that it interest a great number of readers. The story must be true and it must give rise to a new thought or present a new problem to constitute an acceptable news item.

Review Questions.

1. What four requisites are necessary to the writing of successful news stories?
2. What is meant by the expression "nose for news?"
3. Why must the correspondent always be accurate in his reports?
4. What are some of the subjects that make news? Can you point out a reason for the news' value of each?
5. Sum up as briefly as possible the requirements necessary to make any happening into a news story.

Lesson III.

NEWS SOURCES.

It is quite as important for a correspondent to know where news is most likely to be found as it is for him to be able to recognize a news story when he finds it. He may have an idea that correspondents are paid to wander about town waiting and hoping that a truck will run over someone, or that a woman will open a window and yell "Fire!" If so, he is mistaken. Were newspapers compelled to have correspondents patrolling the streets in order to gather stories, the cost of collecting news would be prohibitive.

While a newspaper has comparatively few salaried men on its staff of reporters and correspondents, it has hundreds of observers who are not paid, and yet who are always on the alert for news material. Perhaps most useful among these are the police. Every policeman is obliged to make a complete report to his captain of every fire, robbery, accident, murder, or any occurrence involving loss of life or property, or the endangering of life or property, on his beat. This report is made to the local precinct station and from there is 'phoned to police headquarters. At "headquarters" such reports are recorded on the police "blotter," a daily record book. Some of the reports so recorded are withheld from the public, as premature announcement of information gained by the police might warn criminals of impending arrest. But such information as is to be made public is posted on a bulletin board or written in a large book in terse paragraphs or "slips," as they are commonly called. Following are typical slips:

Jan. 21. Ribs Broken.

Thomas Anderson, 29 years, married, 2416 Calumet Ave., truck driver, suffered two broken ribs; horses became frightened at train, B. & O. depot and bolted. Sent to City Hospital by patrol 16.

10:30 A. M. Gorman.

Jan. 23. Injured by Automobile.

Jane Meyerbier, 62 years, widow, 276 S. Cook Street, run down by automobile at 10th and Broad Sts., head and limbs injured. Removed John Street Emergency Hospital, ambulance 7.

3:15 P. M. Olsen.

The name at the lower right-hand corner is that of the patrolman reporting the incident, and the hour noted is the actual time at which the report was received at headquarters.

There are also found at police headquarters records known as "arrest sheets," on which all arrests are noted, and which are available to the public. This is done so that no one be imprisoned unjustly. On these arrest sheets is sufficient information concerning the person apprehended, the charge and complainant, that the correspondent may obtain a brief but accurate account of the accident and crimes in his city. By following these outlines to the source of the event he can procure all the available facts from which to build his news story.

Keep in close touch with the coroner. He receives first information on fatal accidents, suicides, murders, or deaths occurring under suspicious circumstances. Doctors must report to the

authorities on births, deaths and contagious diseases, so should be kept in mind as sources for possible news material.

County Clerks keep records of all marriage licenses issued in their respective counties, while the Recorder of Deeds maintains a register of all sales and transfers of property. Big real-estate deals are always of interest, being eagerly watched for by a great number of readers. The issue of a marriage license, where either person is prominent socially, has news value.

Building Inspectors are points of contact for the news gatherer. From the office of the building inspector are issued permits for the construction of new buildings, while to it come accounts of buildings which are condemned. Hotel registers hold many a story for the alert correspondent who watches them for arrival of important personages in his city.

The acquaintance and friendship of jailors, turnkeys, and wardens of prisons should be cultivated. They sometimes have interesting experiences with notorious law-breakers which are well worth the reading. Many a "thriller" has been brought out of a warden's office by an alert reporter or correspondent.

Prominent business and professional men, club men, and men about town are often in possession of material for a good story. It pays to be friendly with everyone who might by chance help you "scoop" a good story.

The various courts, associated charities, hospitals, political clubs, civic organizations, boards of trade, and chambers of commerce merit attention by the correspondent. Many news items, too, can be gathered at such places as railway offices and depots,

shipping offices, offices of school superintendent, office of public works, S. P. C. A., etc.

Following is a list of the principal news sources and the nature of the news which may be found at each.

Associated Charities Headquarters: destitution, poverty, relief work.

Boards of Trade, Brokers, Commission Men: market quotations, sales of grain, stocks, and bonds; financial outlook.

Boxing Commission: boxing permissions and regulations.

Building Department, Real Estate Dealers, Architects: new buildings, unsafe buildings.

Caterers: banquets, society dinners.

Civic Organizations: reform movements, speakers, etc.

Civil Courts: complaints, trials, decisions.

Commercial Club: business news.

Coroner's Office: fatal accidents, murders, suicides, suspicious deaths.

County Clerk: marriage licenses, county statistics.

County Jail: arrests, crimes, executions.

Criminal Courts: arraignments, trials, verdicts.

Delicatessen Stores: banquets, society dinners.

Fire Department Headquarters: fires, fire losses, fire regulations, condemned buildings.

Florists: banquets, dinners, receptions, social functions.

Health Department: births, deaths, contagious diseases, reports on sanitation.

Hospitals: accidents, illnesses, deaths.

Hotels: important guests, banquets, dinners, social functions.

Morgue: unidentified corpses.

Police Headquarters: accidents, arrests, crimes, fires, lost and found articles, missing persons, suicides, sudden or suspicious deaths.

Political Clubs and Headquarters: county, state, and national political news.

Probate Office: estates, wills.

Public Works Department: civic improvements.

Railway Offices: new rates, general shipping news.

Referee in Bankruptcy: assignments, failures, creditors' meetings, appointments of receivers, settlements.

Register of Deeds: real estate sales and transfers.

Shipping Offices: departure and docking of vessels; cargoes, shipping rates, passenger lists.

Society for the Prevention of Cruelty to Animals: arrests, complaints, animal stories.

Superintendent of Schools: educational news.

Vice Commission: arrests, complaints, raids.

The value of the news sources mentioned in the foregoing paragraphs depends entirely upon the correspondent himself. A certain amount of useful information might be gathered by a school boy, but the correspondent who is alive to his opportunities will strive always to make himself agreeable and useful to those from whom he hopes to receive valuable tips. Not only is this true as regards the police, coroner, firemen, etc., but with reference to everyone he meets--on duty or off. On the streets, on the cars, at the club, the correspondent who is strictly on the job will garner many a good

story. The fight promoter, the merchant, the minister, the private detective, the porter--all make valuable acquaintances who may some time, in some way put you on the trail of a good story. Never, however, betray a confidence. There is a vast difference between publishing the story gained by interviewing a stranger and that secured from a neighbor or friend in confidence. The first must be used by all means, but the second may not be unless permission to do so has first been obtained. It is far better to let a big story go unpublihed by your paper than to send it in to the detriment of your personal and professional honor.

Review Questions.

1. How is news found?
2. What people should the reporter cultivate as acquaintances?
3. Make a list of the most valuable news sources.
4. Should friendships ever be sacrificed for news?

Lesson IV.

HOW TO HANDLE THE STORY.

You have read in the preceding lesson of news sources--places where considerable information might be obtained which could be quickly followed to the scene of the occúrrence and details secured from which the story is built. The correspondent's situation changes rapidly, however, when he is simply told that someone has been shot at 56th and Grant avenue. The shooting may have occurred at any of the four corners. If some of these houses are apartments, the matter is still more complicated.

If the name of the person shot has been given you, look it up in the telephone book or city directory to obtain some idea of the man and his profession. Do not try to reach his residence and obtain the story by telephone, as it is too easy for the person answering to hang up the receiver in order to avoid publicity. Furthermore, the facial expressions and gestures, often indicating guilt or innocence, cannot be seen. Use the telephone only in confirming rumors or running down tips, or for obtaining stories that the persons concerned wish to appear in the paper. In the case above set forth, visit the scene of the shooting for your story.

On your arrival at 56th and Grant avenue, you should go first to the policeman on the beat. Unless the shooting has for some reason been hushed up, you can obtain principal details from the officer. As a usual thing, if properly approached, he will point out the house where the shooting occurred and tell all he knows. If the patrolman knows nothing, or pretends to be ignorant of the details, you must go to the house itself, to the adjoining residences, to neighboring

stores. Do not become discouraged if you fail to get information at the scene of the shooting or at several nearby houses; keep inquiring and questioning until you have exhausted every source. There is no story that cannot be obtained in some way, and the stories which are difficult to get, are usually the really big ones. Inquire of the children playing in the block; telephone to the leading hospitals (and here is where acquaintanceship of doctors is valuable); inquire at corner houses in adjoining blocks. In any event, do not give up until you have investigated every available clue. Your paper or press association wants news--not excuses.

It may be that at the last place where you inquire you will get the story or learn where the victim lives. You may find that he was only slightly injured, or the person answering the door may tell you that Mr. Blank cannot be seen, as he was injured. Your next step would be to express regret at learning of Mr. Blank's injury and to inquire the cause. In this manner you could open an interview in a natural way.

Interviewing, the most exacting of all correspondent's duties, requires a pleasing personality, an even temper, a quick recognition of news values, (even in chance remarks), a retentive memory and the power to recognize statements which are not true. You cannot expect to be well received if you are unshaven, or your apparel isn't spic and span; nor can you look for consideration from the person interviewed, if you do not approach your subject tactfully. Flattery isn't tact, and the chances are the one you interview is just as keen as yourself, and will not be moved by mere flattery to tell you what you wish to learn.

Tactfulness in questioning often determines the success or failure of the news-gatherer, because many of the big stories are lost or won by the impression made in the early moments of the interview. It is always safe to put yourself in the place of the man you are interviewing; ask yourself what you would be interested in if a newspaper man approached you. You'd probably answer, "my work or my hobby." Then, isn't it likely that the person interviewed would be receptive if approached from that angle? It may at times be necessary to guide the conversation to the subject on which you wish to question, but it is far better to do this when you are on a friendly basis with your man than to attempt a frontal attack which means almost certain failure.

The late Richard Harding Davis once said: "They (reporters and correspondents) become stars because they observe things that other people miss and do not let it appear that they have observed them. When the great man who is being interviewed blurts out that which is indiscrete but most important, the cub says: 'That's most interesting, sir. I'll make a note of that.' And so warns the great man into silence. But the star receives the indiscrete utterance as though it bored him; and the great man does not know he has blundered until he reads of it the next morning under screaming headlines."

It is for such cases that the correspondent requires ability to perceive news value in a statement, for if he does not grasp it immediately, he may give himself away when he realizes its importance; or he may forget it altogether.

Here, too, is where a retentive memory is essential. Many persons grow alarmed at the sight of a note book or copy paper, and will

not talk, while others grow cautious when they realize that what they say is being recorded word for word. The correspondent should hold firmly in his mind the facts learned during the interview, and as soon as it is closed, hurry to a place where he can make his notes.

Since the purpose of an interview is to gather facts from which a story may be built, the correspondent must be able to distinguish the true from the false statements made by the person interviewed. All persons who consent to be interviewed, or who answer questions even though refusing a so-called interview, talk with a purpose. Sometimes they do so to advance their own interests, and sometimes to injure another's. In many instances they speak truthfully, but occasionally--especially when a man holds a grudge against another--they prevaricate. It is an established fact, too, that few persons can render an uncolored account of even the most common-place event. This frequently arises from excitement at the time of the occurrence; or, it may be brought about by prejudice against persons involved. To make the most of his opportunities, therefore, a correspondent must be capable of judging the mental attitude of those interviewed and make allowances for motives which might prompt them to act and speak as they do. The man you are interviewing may be nursing animosity against his neighbor because the neighbor's chickens ruined his garden, or the neighbor's daughter plays the piano late at night and interferes with his sleep. A good many libel suits might have been avoided had the correspondents or reporters detected falsehood readily.

For this very reason it is not advisable to accept the word of one person to support your story. Better, by far, question everyone

connected with the happening than risk-making trouble for your paper. Interview as many people as possible who were in any way connected with the affair. Often a janitor, a porter or a child can give important information, and--by the way--children generally speak the truth because they have no prejudices. Learn as much as possible about the past history of the person involved. If the man has served a prison term, or the woman has been divorced, or if any of the persons have been in the public eye, such information will serve to identify the characters in your story.

In short, get every detail that you can obtain, from every source you can approach, before quitting. It is much easier to discard material that you have gathered than to go back for additional information which you neglected.

Review Questions.

1. What are some of the difficulties that the reporter fares in following a "tip?"
2. Should the reporter ever give up?
3. What qualities are necessary to be a successful interviewer?
4. Why should news stories always be carefully verified?

writing. Accuracy, conciseness and clearness are indispensable, of course; but any correspondent's work has these characteristics. If you want to hew a way for yourself at the top of your profession, put YOURSELF into your stories by individuality of expression and style.

Keep on the alert for the "local end" of stories, both by picking up leads in your home town and by watching the metropolitan papers. For example: President Harding (or other nationally prominent man) has a cousin visiting in your city; notorious bandit, Harry Starr, killed in attempted hold-up of express car, once worked in local restaurant. Localize your news in every possible way. In this, as in all phases of a correspondent's work, wide acquaintanceship is immensely valuable. If you haven't it, cultivate it. Use your friendship with a few prominent persons to enlarge your circle. Get interviews from local persons of importance regarding big problems of national, state and civic interest. Don't ask for an interview. Engage your man in conversation and adroitly bring up the subject on which you desire his opinion. Do not attempt to make notations while conducting an interview, or you may lose your story. Here, of course, is where a retentive memory is valuable, since you must wait until the interview is closed before writing your story.

Certain tools are necessary to correspondents. Chief among these is the telephone. When you learn of an occurrence of importance, it is quicker and easier to get the story over the 'phone than to risk missing an edition by waiting until you've visited the scene of the incident. Use a city map. It's helpful in spotting locations quickly. Carry several pencils and plenty of folded copy paper for note taking. Keep your pencils and note paper out of sight as much

as possible. People talk more freely when questioned, if you seem to be only casually interested. Rely on your memory in order to get the notes later. Some persons believe that cards are necessary for correspondents and reporters. This is a mistake. As a matter of fact, they may prove to be a disadvantage when improperly employed.

Tact is a vital factor in the game of news gathering, and when a correspondent does not possess this attribute in marked degree, is should be assiduously cultivated. For example: Anyone could go into a court room and get the news of a trial by behaving with ordinary decorum, but to get into the private office of a big corporation official and come away with the story of a momentous industrial event in advance of rival papers (a scoop)--that requires tact.

Do not confuse tact with deception. You may be adroit and tactful without being untruthful. On occasion you may find it necessary to misrepresent your occupation as, for instance, passing yourself off as an official in order to secure the story of a crime. Never betray a confidence no matter how you may be tempted. You wield a great power as an arm of the press; don't abuse it under any circumstances. Verify all stories before sending them to your paper. To fail in this regard may subject your paper to a suit for libel. If you are in doubt as to the authenticity of a story and are unable to check it in detail, do not send it in. Never fake a story, even in part. Leave personal feeling out of your work and do not allow prejudice to prompt you in wilfully distorting facts.

Vigilance is as important in a correspondent as it is to the observer on a submarine-hunting destroyer. You must live your work all the time--eating, sleeping or playing, news should be in the

forefront of your mind. Hard work, persistence and untiring energy always win. Trail a tip as a bloodhound follows a scent. More often than not the story is there. Hang on like a bulldog until you get it.

Keep yourself immaculate in appearance. You are representing a publication that takes pride in the appearance of its editions. As its ambassador, you should be neat, clean-shaven and supplied with clean linen on all occasions--in short, truly representative.

Be uniformly courteous to persons you meet, regardless of their walk in life. If it doesn't come natural to you, cultivate the habit. You can't tell when a lowly newsboy may be in position to "tip you off" to the story of your life. As stated previously, you should make friends wherever possible. To do that you must be human--courteous, friendly and generally likeable.

If you are in good bealth you probably have a good memory. A retentive memory is important to successful news gathering, and must be painstakingly developed where disuse has rendered the memory poor. In interviewing a person you cannot expect him to talk unrestrainedly, if you are taking notes. You should cultivate your memory until you can remember the outstanding details of a story long after the interview. Of course, there are exceptions. For example: scientific men often want their ideas expressed verbatim; engineers and technical men give out figures of building projects; army or navy construction experts report dimensions of artillery equipment or naval craft. In such cases it is essential that you take notes.

In reporting on lectures it is generally possible to obtain advance copies of speeches. You can usually secure free tickets for such events, oftentimes for a seat at a table close by the platform.

Where feasible, get photographs of speakers. It is well to remember that the spirit of the address is of greater importance than the actual spoken words. Your paper or syndicate depends upon you to catch the spirit and put it in news form.

Too great care cannot be exercised in order to secure absolute accuracy in your articles, especially as to names, descriptions, street addresses, etc. Read over your copy thoroughly before sending it to your paper; if necessary, verify names and addresses. A misspelled name, misplaced word, or even an accidental resemblance between names or between personal descriptions often causes libel suits. Not only does this reflect discredit upon you and your paper, but, under the law governing libel, you as well as the publication may be held for damages. Any published matter, that tends to degrade a person, or that may be construed in that light, is generally considered libelous.

Qualify your statements wherever you can, saying, for example: "It is alleged that Smith shot Brown after a quarrel over cards;" "It is said that Jones was sent to, etc;" "It is charged that Williams robbed the First National Bank at, etc." Limiting or qualifying phrases such as these take your statements out of the class of positive accusations.

A common failing among correspondents is a tendency to editorialize--to write in the first person as though they were voicing the opinion of the paper. Beware of this stumbling block, which is the sign of the novice. To illustrate: Don't say, "Outrages of this nature are becoming all too common," but "In the opinion of many leading citizens, outrages of this nature, etc." Better yet, omit entirely and give only actual facts.

Condense the matter in your stories. Boil them down so that the tale is told in simple, direct style. Newspaper space is valuable and it is important that superfluous words be eliminated. In writing any story, ask yourself what facts would interest you as a reader of the paper and confine yourself to those facts. To illustrate, take a fire: (1) What was destroyed? (2) Where located? (3) What damage was incurred? (4) What occupants, women, children? (5) the Time? (6) The cause? (7) What made loss possible? (8) What amount of insurance? (9) How was fire discovered? (10) How did it spread? (11) When was alarm given? Feature remarkable escapes, list of dead or injured, or act of heroism--if any.

Write plain, forceful English. Avoid stereotyped phrases, stock expressions and slang such as: John D, Old Sol, cold in death, oil king, fatal noose, dull thud, fought like a tiger, hurled into eternity, last sad rites, dark horse, blushing bride, appeared on the scene, large and enthusiastic audience, doing as well as can be expected. Do not attempt crude or affected psychology, or any form of so-called "fine writing." Write simple facts in the order of their importance and in language that the reader can easily understand. Remember that newspapers publish news for ALL the masses, and while well-educated persons can grasp simple language, those with little education cannot and will not read stories which are "over their heads."

Review Questions.

1. What is the general style that must be followed in all news stories? What makes this necessary?
2. What is meant by the "local end" of stories? How does it increase the story's value?
3. What are the correspondents' main tools?
4. What is meant by qualifying statements? Why should this be done?
5. What is a good plan to follow in determining the gist of a story?

Lesson VI.

NEWSPAPER CORRESPONDENCE.

The style and construction of correspondence stories is no different from the style and construction of the news stories heretofore described. The same general rules govern the handling of a story that is to be printed by a nearby paper as those which are destined for a publication or great press syndicate a hundred or more miles away. Yet there is a vast difference in the relative value of news items, which is affected by the locality in which they are to appear. An event which, because of the local prominence of the persons connected with it, is of sufficient importance for a first-page story, would be worth only a few lines in a paper published a hundred miles away. The viewpoint of the reader, then, must be your viewpoint in determining the value of the news story. If you are "covering" your town for a press association, you must understand that only happenings of national interest are worthy of big space. For example: A daring aviator, whose flights have focused the eyes of the nation on him, falls and is killed near your town in attempting to break the New York to San Francisco record; A youngster who was kidnapped and whose disappearance caused activity on the part of police and detectives all over the country, is found in your town; any incident of news value that has to do with a person or persons of national fame.

To appreciate the importance of the small town and country press, it must be understood that approximately 20,000 of the 25,000 newspapers in the United States are country papers, either county

dailies or weekly papers. It is from the reporters on these small publications that the leading dailies in the large towns and cities obtain their state and sectional news. These country correspondents, by the way, make our metropolitan reporters, editors, sport writers, special writers, and feature writers. A reporter on one of these numerous small-town papers may write a column or more in covering a fire in the business section of the little place. He will go into detail as to occupants of the stores and offices in the building which was destroyed; the loss of each person or concern and how much was covered by insurance. He may even mention the name of each fireman who responded to the alarm. All this detail because readers of newspapers in small communities know almost everyone in the town and every one is interested in anything concerning the other. Yet, when this same reporter, acting as correspondent for a big city daily or a great press association, sends in the story of that fire to the larger publication, it will probably read: "Fire which destroyed the Hamilton Building, Brookville, Monday night, resulted in damage estimated at $50,000, partially covered by insurance." The reason for this abbreviated statement is that the readers of the metropolitan newspaper who see the story are not interested particularly in what happens in Brookville unless it is something far out of the ordinary.

In addition to these country reporter-correspondents, every large daily paper has its representatives in the chief cities of the country, who, while often engaged in regular reporting, do work of a correspondence nature also. In a strict sense these representatives are detailed on special assignments, just as though they were in their home city; but they are correspondents inasmuch as they work without

the supervision or direction of an editor. Therefore, they must be discriminating in judging news. In one direction, the correspondent-representative of the big-city paper has a decided advantage over his country cousin, since he has naturally a wider field and, therefore, a greater bulk of news material from which to choose. On the other hand, he must decide and quickly, too, what news is of interest to his paper and its readers situated hundreds of miles away. His decisions must be made quickly because he is always in competition with the representatives of one or more rival papers published in his home town. The rivalry in such a situation is just as great as that which exists in the town where the papers are published, where the contending reporters are always on the look-out for a "scoop" or "beat." When competition among representative-correspondents is so keen it is generally the man who is always alert and on the job, or who has the largest acquaintance, who carries off the bulk of the honors.

In the general run of cases, do not send your paper purely local news, unless you happen to represent a county paper in a small community. In other words, do not send to a paper miles away, news items that are of interest only in your own circumscribed locality. We have in mind such stories as burglaries, obituaries, marriages, entertainments, robberies, minor accidents, court trials of little-known persons, murders of obscure people unless there is something unusual about the circumstances attending them, mystery surrounding them, etc. Do not send stories of county fairs, fraternal meetings or entertainments, stories that trespass the limits of good taste or decency, press-agent stories of any kind, or anything savoring of local gossip.

Investigate carefully sensational stories of whatever nature before sending them to your paper. If the rumor came from a source you consider reliable and the story is not libelous, you may send it prefixed with, "It is rumored that," and add to your wire: "The story is being investigated." You cannot be too careful in this respect. If in doubt as to whether your story may be construed as libelous, and you cannot substantiate the information given you, by all means drop it. Suits for libel are serious both to the paper and the correspondent, causing unfavorable comment, embarrassment, and needless expense for the paper, and possibly for the correspondent as well, who under the law is subject to action for libel.

Any correspondent can easily ascertain what his paper desires in the way of news by reading the publication--by studying it assiduously. Some publications want freak news, happenings that are tinged with the unusual and the mysterious, such as strange disappearances; some prefer stories of sport and athletics; others show a taste for scandal, "divorce proceedings threatened," or "bank cashier suspected of embezzlement, found short in accounts;" many want human interest stories--those that play on the heartstrings of the reader, including the so-called sob-stories, as "Dog Gives Up Life to Save Master" or "Aged Man Learns On Death Bed of Fortune Due Him." Still other publications desire news stories of an educational nature, developments of interest in science, art, music, literature, industry commerce and politics.

It is important that you send photographs as well as news in covering a story of exceptional interest, and the bigger the story, the more reason for the photos to illustrate it. Get in the habit of

securing photographs with your stories wherever possible, so that when a big one comes along you'll get them automatically. Of course, if the big story covers an event that may be anticipated, your paper or syndicate in all probability will send a special man and a photographer to work with you in covering the assignment. It is a good idea, however, for you to work always as though you expected to have no help, and thus become self-reliant, vigilant and resourceful. Then when, in an emergency such as the sudden "breaking" of a big story, your paper or association cannot get help to you in time to be of assistance, you can cover the event independently. Many a correspondent has come from obscurity under a condition such as described above. It is well worth the patience and hard work and time expended, if, when the great opportunity comes, you find yourself in position to grasp it and handle the situation with credit.

In sending a news story to your paper do not hesitate to use the wire or special delivery stamps. If a story is worth printing at all it is worth getting in the first edition you are able to reach by the shortest route, so send it by telegraph if a special delivery stamp isn't quick enough. Your news matter must be in the hands of the editor not later than 9:30 or 10:00 a. m. for an evening paper, and not later than 9:00 p. m. for a morning paper. In all cases and under all conditions keep in close touch with the State Editor, Assistant State Editor, or with whomever you are associated, and obey instructions. The kind of work you are doing at a particular time largely determines the member of the editorial staff to whom you should report, as, for example, in covering a big athletic event, you would probably work in conjunction with the sporting editor.

Opportunities come to the correspondent who is ever on the alert, ever preparing for them, and determined to make the most of his chances, demonstrating his ability to do bigger things by handling little assignments in a big way. You may be located in a small town and may have to wait a long time before a really big story "breaks" in your community. When it does, make the most of it. It may be a million-dollar fire, a disastrous storm, a great flood, the construction of important public works, the coming to town of a notable, a murder, etc. Whatever it is, play it to the very limit for the sake of your paper or association, for the sake of your pocketbook, and also for the sake of the advancement which brilliant handling of such stories usually brings. Talent able to handle big stories under the stress of an emergency is not so plentiful that the real worth of one's services is likely to be overlooked. But it must be remembered that ability to handle first-page stories creditably comes only through hard work and persistent effort in the right direction. You cannot expect to pursue your daily work in half-hearted fashion and then achieve brilliant results in the handling of a big news story. There is no royal road to fame and fortune in correspondence any more than in other lines of endeavor. Indefatigable energy and love of the game alone will bring measurable success and increased pay.

Stories in advance of leading events are acceptable to most publications and syndicates, and, in fact, are welcomed. Like other important stories, they should, wherever possible, be accompanied by photographs of places, buildings, notable persons, etc. Ask yourself what illustrations you would want to see and you will know what photos to secure.

Avoid transmitting stories over telephone. It is not only slow and costly, but involves unnecessary work on the part of the paper as well as yourself. It requires that you have your story already written, and your newspaper must have a stenographer at the other end of the wire to take notes. In spite of the exercise of great care, inaccuracies will creep in and spoil a good story. As a general rule send your stories by telegraph or mail. It is often the case that telegrams are faster in the long run, and undoubtedly they are less likely to be wrongly interpreted.

Above all, don't be miserly about employing whatever means may come to hand in order to get a story to the publication in time for a certain edition. Use an automobile--even an airplane--if necessary, in order to save time. What to you may seem exorbitant expenses, are incidentals to great metropolitan newspapers. They want the news at all hazards and they want it while it is news-- not after it has become stale. It is better for your paper and more to your credit to score a scoop by making a fifty-mile run on a motorcycle, even though you have to buy the motorcycle, than it is to have rival papers beat you to the story. If there is a doubt in your mind as to the real worth of a story, do not hold or delay it, but query your editor somewhat after this fashion:

> "First National Bank burns; loss quarter-million; fully covered; incendiarism suspected; police working on clew; three hundred."

This is a specimen query, and you will generally get an answer asking for the three hundred words, or possibly less; or the editor may use your outline of the story for an early edition--especially a "bull-dog"--that might go to your city. In any event you will have covered

your story and drawn the favorable attention of your editor to your work.

In sending news stories by telegraph, never skeletonize your text by omitting a's, the's, on's, is's, etc. The small saving effected is in reality not a saving at all since it is more than offset by the additional time and expense required in editing when it reaches the office. Associated Press news, and the stories of other press associations, are sent complete to the member-papers and, at times are condensed more often than amplified in the offices of the papers. Under no circumstances are "articles" or other parts of speech omitted to save tolls.

It is well to secure from your paper rules for correspondents, especially those governing the closing of editions. In most cases these can be obtained in printed or typewritten form, or they may be had in a letter from the state editor, telegraph editor, Sunday or feature editor of the publication. Always bear in mind, however, that on really big stories you have unusual privileges. All rules are suspended when an unusual story breaks. For example, if you are busy on an important story and haven't time to write it so as to reach your paper, you may wire at the last minute and start your story on the wire, keeping installments coming as fast as you can write them. In a case of this kind the presses will be held or an extra edition published. This method of procedure is to be used only in emergencies and in connection with stories of great import. It should not be made an excuse for delaying a big story until too late to reach an edition, as it costs tremendous sums of money to hold up an edition or to publish an extra. (Courtesy "NEWS WRITING," Spencer.)

Review Questions.

1. What is the difference between a reporter and a correspondent?
2. What are the happenings that the correspondent must watch for?
3. Where do you find correspondents? What opportunities are ahead of the correspondent?
4. How can the correspondent determine the type of news required by "his paper?"
5. Of what importance are photographs?
6. How should stories be forwarded to the paper?

Lesson VII.

HOW TO HANDLE "COPY".

Manuscript which is prepared for printing is called "copy". It is written according to the rules of the newspaper. If you are acting as correspondent for a paper, ask for the style book, which is printed for the guidance of reporters, copy-readers, compositors and correspondents. It is quite possible that your paper may have no such book, as only the big metropolitan dailies print their style rules, and you will have to study the columns of the paper and the changes made in printing your own stories. If the paper does print a style book, you should spend every spare moment familiarizing yourself with the rules and write every story strictly in accordance with them. Copy readers insist on strict observance of the regulations, and they must be observed even though some of them appear absurd.

Learn to operate a typewriter. Stories written in longhand sometimes come into a newspaper office, but in such cases it is often given to a stenographer to copy. There may be times when, for the sake of speed in transmission of a story to the paper, it appears best to send longhand copy. In such an event, write with painstaking care for accuracy. Unusual proper names, or technical names not familiar to laymen, are apt to be misread and should be printed. Use a small cross at the end of a sentence instead of a period.

As a general thing newspapers supply copy paper and return envelopes to correspondents. In case where they fail to, select an unglazed paper of white or yellow--unruled sheets 6x9 or 8½x11 inches

in size--and of sufficient strength to permit the use of ink or pencil.

Leave the top half of the first page blank so the headline writer may write headlines there. Also leave a margin of not less than one inch at bottom and each side of every page. All except the first page should have one-inch margin at the top. The side margins are for the editor's convenience in correcting copy, while the top and bottom spaces allow room for pasting the sheets together.

Indent all paragraphs an inch and mark the beginning of each with the rectangle (L) sign. If two paragraphs have been run together through an oversight, insert the paragraph sign (¶) immediately before the word beginning the new paragraph and write the same symbol in the margin. Should the paragraph complete the page, this same symbol should be marked at the end to show the compositor his "take" with a broken line. When you find it necessary to consolidate two paragraphs that have been written separately, draw a line from the end of the first to the beginning of the second and mark "No ¶" in the margin. This same method may be employed where several lines have been scratched out and the matter is meant to be continuous.

Do not crowd your work. Adjust your typewriter to make triple spaces between lines. If you find it necessary to write the copy in longhand leave at least a quarter-inch space between lines. Crowded lines cause much extra work for copy readers, compelling them to cut and paste many times in making corrections. The only exception to this rule is where you have a paragraph which is a bit too long for the page. It is better to crowd the last lines a trifle rather than run a few words over to a new page. Where a

paragraph would normally begin on the last line of a page, leave the line blank and start the paragraph on a new page. Never write on both sides of a sheet, as copy is cut up into "takes" in the newspaper office, each "take" going to a different compositor. Number your pages at the top with an Arabic--not a Roman--numeral and enclose in a circle so it may not be mistaken for a part of the article.

Make just as few corrections as possible. Where any insertion or alteration of considerable size is necessary, write it on another sheet, cut the sheet where it is to be inserted and paste it in. Do not by any means write it in the margins.

When a story is not complete either because the end of the sheet has been reached or because more of the story is to follow, write the word "more" in a circle at the foot of the page. The circle is used so that the compositor will not mistake the word "more" for a part of the copy.

Underscore words once for italics, twice for small capitals, and three times for capitals, and use wave-line underscoring for display type. Indicate as nearly as possible the location of cuts or illustrations to appear in your story by marking the place "Turn rule for cut," thus telling the compositor to set a ruled line in the story where a cut is to appear. The position of the cut may be changed by the make-up man to obtain a better balance of illustrations on the page or to avoid placing the picture where the paper will fold, but the direction is useful in placing the illustration accurately. Clippings used in the story should be pasted--not pinned or clipped--in the copy. If pinned or clipped, they are likely to become lost.

When it is necessary to eliminate words or letters from copy,

paragraph would normally begin on the last line of a page, leave the line blank and start the paragraph on a new page. Never write on both sides of a sheet, as copy is cut up into "takes" in the newspaper office, each "take" going to a different compositor. Number your pages at the top with an Arabic numeral [illegible] a circle so it may not be mistaken for a part of the article.

Make just as few corrections as possible. [illegible]

draw a line through them with a pen. Then draw a line between those to be set up together. It will not do to enclose in parentheses words you wish eliminated, as the compositor will set them up, parentheses and all. Should you strike out a word through error and wish to restore it to the copy, place a series of dots below it and write "stet" in the margin. The word "stet" means "leave stand." To transpose two words, letters or phrases, draw a continuous line over the first and under the second and write "tr" in the margin. A capital letter that should have been a lower case or small letter may be indicated by drawing a diagonal line downward from right to left through the letter. Abbreviations and figures which are to be spelled out are often indicated by drawing a ring around them. Care should be exercised, however, so that no figures or abbreviations are ringed unless you wish them spelled out in full. It is easier for a copy reader to ring a number than to erase a ring unnecessarily made. Where it is necessary to set up misspelled, slangy or ungrammatical copy, or poorly punctuated sentences--as in case of a dialect, story, or in quoting a speaker--mark in the margin "Follow Copy."

Designate the end of your story with two or three marks #. Then read the copy from start to finish very carefully, correcting every error, no matter how slight. Then send the copy to your paper, unfolded if possible. Never roll copy. If it is absolutely necessary to fold it for mailing, fold lengthwise. Folding copy crosswise makes it hard to handle. Do not pin the sheets together--paste them.

Read your stories carefully after they have appeared in type, noting carefully where changes have been made in your copy. This is the best way to discover your mistakes and correct them. By watching

and comparing the rough copy and printed story you can see what is expected of you and improve your style of writing.

The folowing are marks used in correcting copy and those used by proof readers:

amb = Ambiguous.

and = A bad "and" sentence. Make two sentences or subordinate one clause.

ant = Antecedent not clear.

Cl = Not clear.

Cst = Construction faulty.

Coh = Coherence not good.

Con = Wrong connective.

Del = Delete.

dull = Dull reading; put more life into the story.

E = Error.

ed = Editorializing; too much personal opinion.

FW = "Fine writing."

Gr = Bad grammar.

K = Awkward; clumsily expressed.

ld = Poor lead; revise.

P = Punctuation wrong.

pt = Point of view shifted.

qt = Make this a direct quotation

rep = Same word repeated too much.

rew = Rewrite.

sent = Use shorter sentences.

Sl = Slang.

Sp = Bad spelling.

SU = Sentence lacks unity.

T = Wrong tense.

unnec = Unnecessary details; omit some of them.

tr = Transpose.

W = Wrong use of word.

? = Truth of statement questioned.

¶ = Begin a new paragraph.

No = No paragraph needed.

□ = Indent.

= = Put the words together as one.

= Separate into two words.

- = Hyphen needed.

Review Questions.

1. What is "copy"?
2. What rules should be followed in preparing all copy?
3. Study this chapter carefully again. Neatness and accuracy always reach the attention of those higher up and affect the correspondent's chances for a bigger job to a great extent.

Lesson VIII.

GENERAL INSTRUCTIONS.

There are certain fundamental rules of procedure that you should study until they are as much a part of your working paraphernalia as your pencils and note paper, for they are quite as important in the successful handling of your duties.

1. When forwarding to your paper or association time stories, advance manuscripts of speeches, photographs, etc., send them by mail; never by express. Express companies do not deliver at night.

2. In telegrams always spell out round numbers, and mark the beginning of speeches "quote" and the ending "quote".

3. Keep the telegraph companies informed of your street address and telephone number so they will know at all times where to reach you. It is also well to maintain friendly relations with telegraph operators as they can frequently be of valuable service to you.

4. When a big story breaks, or you get a tip that one is about to break, go after it. Even though there is need for incurring expense, get the story, as newspapers will stand for any reasonable expense for valuable news. In regard to this matter of tips, the number of these you receive will depend largely upon the extent of your acquaintanceship. Therefore, do not lose an opportunity to make a new friend or a new acquaintance. Each new addition to your list is "water on your wheel." You cannot tell when Banker Smith, or Councilman Case, is going to be able to tip you off to a big story.

5. Never overlook the value of sending time stories. Every

minute is valuable. Every minute wasted gives some rival newspaper or news service an opportunity to beat you into print with the story. It is infinitely preferable to send a short sketch of the story by wire and follow it with the complete article in installments than it is to risk the loss of the scoop. Keep always in the forefront of your mind the fact that your story is news only as long as it is fresh.

You cannot make too many friends and acquaintances if you are engaged in correspondence work. The humblest bootblack may be the means of putting you on the trail of the biggest story of the year. Become friendly with everybody from the night watchman at the bank to the court bailiff, and from the train caller at the Union Station to the District Attorney. All of them can be of help to you in some way, at some time. Many reporters and correspondents go out of their way to cultivate the friendship of officials at police headquarters, detectives and private operatives, as in this way they are sure to get the first tip of big events of a criminal nature. While the "blotter" at police headquarters is available to newspaper men, and they can pick up additional information from policemen, other correspondents and reporters can avail themselves of these sources as well. By becoming friendly with detectives who are working on big cases you may be in position to score a scoop for your paper by being on the ground early.

It is not amiss to emphasize again the value of courtesy in the every-day life of a correspondent. You cannot expect people to favor you unless they like you, and they won't like you unless you are courteous and considerate of their feelings.

The correspondent who works by the golden rule will be well

repaid. If you treat people that you meet in your daily work with consideration and courtesy, you are likely to receive the same sort of treatment in return. Never forget that you are a gentleman, regardless of the actions of the person you are interviewing. In the work you are undertaking you cannot afford to get angry--it doesn't pay you and it certainly works against the best interest of your publication or association. When you become angry you lose command of the situation because your mind is on the affront put upon you instead of on your business. You are so absorbed in your own real or fancied wrongs that you cannot question your man to any purpose, nor can you remember after the interview what he has told you. A display of temper cannot be indulged in by a correspondent who hopes to be successful and reach higher planes in his chosen field. It rears a wall of hostility between you and the man or woman from whom you seek information, and after that you can be sure no information will be forthcoming voluntarily. Besides, when you become angry, with or without cause, you create an enemy for your paper. Be courteous and gentlemanly under all provocations; maintain a cheerful, kindly attitude in spite of irritability of the person interviewed. In the long run, he will yield to your mood. If some other paper has already printed the story, its value to your paper is reduced ninety per cent. Quick thinking and quick acting will turn the trick.

6. Until you have received your first check, clip and preserve every one of your stories that is printed. This for the sake of your pocketbook. Most newspapers as well as the press association keep their own accounts with correspondents, but there are some which require you to send in at the end of the month your

"string"--that is, all the stories you have written during the month pasted together, end to end. Payment is then made on the basis of the number of columns printed, the rates varying from $2.00 to $7.00 a column of 1500 words.

As every paper has different rules for correspondents, apply for printed or typewritten copy when you undertake your duties. If your paper has not printed or typewritten rules, you must study the news columns and follow the style and arrangement indicated. While gathering news for a paper located at a distant point, a correspondent must always regard himself as a reporter and write his stories in the form in which they are to appear in print if he wishes to be a correspondent for a long time. The following "Instructions to Correspondents" are sent out on a printed card to correspondents of the St. Louis Star:

> QUERY BY WIRE ON ALL STORIES you consider are worth telegraphing, unless you are absolutely certain The Star wants you to send the story without query, or in case of a big story breaking suddenly near edition time. If you have no time to query, get a reply and send such matter as might be ordered before the next edition time; send the story in the shortest possible number of words necessary to tell it, asking if additional matter is desired.
>
> Write your queries so they can be understood. Never send a "blind" query. If John Smith, a confirmed bachelor, whose age is 80 years, elopes with and marries the daughter of the woman who jilted him when he was a youth, say so in as few words as possible, but be sure to convey the dramatic news worth of the

story in your query. Do not say, "Bachelor elopes with girl, daughter of woman he knew a long time ago." In itself the story which this query tells might be worth printing, but it would not be half so good a story as the elopment of John Smith, 80, bachelor, woman hater, with the daughter of his old sweetheart.

When a good story breaks close to edition time and the circumstances justify it, use the long-distance telephone, but first be reasonably certain The Star will not get the story from another source.

Write your stories briefly. The Star desires to remunerate its correspondents according to the worth of a story and not for so many words. One good story of 200 words with the right "punch" in the introduction is worth a dozen strung over as many dozen pages of copy paper with the real story in the last paragraph of each. Tell your story in simple, every-day conversational words; quit when you have finished. Relegate the details. Unless it is a case of identification in a murder mystery, or some similar big story, no one cares about the color of the man's hair. Get the principal facts in the first paragraph --stop soon after.

Send as much of your stuff as possible by mail, especially if you have the story in the late afternoon and are near enough to St. Louis to rech The Star by 9 o'clock the next morning. If necessary, send the letter special delivery.

Don't stop working on a good story when you have all the facts; if there are photographs to be obtained, get the photographs, especially if the principals in the story are persons of standing, and more especially if they are women.

Correspondents will appreciably increase their worth to The Star and enhance their earning capacity by observing these rules.

Appended hereto is a copy of rules for correspondents issued by the Cincinnati Times Star, which will enable you to familiarize yourself with the requirements of big-city dailies in general:

We are much interested in having you cover thoroughly for us the news of your county or special news district, both by mail and wire. (1) Let news about Cincinnatians and any news having a direct connection with them or with Cincinnati interests hold the first place in your consideration as it does in ours. (2) News of general interest is always in demand--but be sure that it is of general interest. (3) Matters of importance to your city, county and state come third. This should be of importance not only to your local people, but also of some special interest to others. It must NOT be routine local news.

No matter in what class the news falls, it must be most concisely worded, whether sent by mail or by wire. We should be queried about any news that seems to be of special importance and worth more than a brief statement. The query should be so worded that we may use it alone, if we are not in a position at the time to order more. Please always indicate about how many words a complete story of the matter would require. Should we use nothing but the query, we will liberally credit you for that.

We are glad to receive by mail advance stories and minor

items and even more important news when you are certain that the news is exclusive.

Should news develop after 12 noon, make virtually only a bulletin of it. We can always order more if we can use more. We can use these bulletins up to 4:30 p. m., provided they are IN THE OFFICE at that time.

Never wire more than the briefest query about night-before news unless you are certain that it was not sent to the morning papers, here or elsewhere.

Remember that the Times-Star is an EVENING paper and is NOT published on Sunday. Matter may be wired at night when you are certain that the morning papers will not have it.

A story that reaches us before noon is worth much more than one that comes later. The quicker the news reaches us the better for everybody, including yourself.

We want the news QUICKLY, ACCURATELY, CONCISELY, and EARLY.

We do not want deaths or marriages of unimportant persons, ordinary fires, small thefts or the insignificant crimes or matters of exclusively local interest.

SEND US NO LONG STORY EXCEPT IN RESPONSE TO ORDERS.

Do not "skeletonize." Give the full names of rail-roads, etc.

Query us about news outside your particular territory when you have good reason to believe that you have it exclusively.

Pictures of persons, places and events that have news

value, are always desired, should be mailed promptly, and will be paid for liberally when used, or promptly returned. We gladly return all pictures, the return of which is requested. Should there be expense involved in sending pictures, please consult us in advance, by mail or wire, stating what the pictures are and what the expense will be. You may safely send us immediately any pictures of IMPORTANT NEWS VALUE.

We are always open to suggestions and eager to co-operate with you. If there is anything you don't understand, let us explain it. We consider you a valuable part of our regular news staff and want you so to consider yourself.

The following is taken from a list of instructions furnished correspondents by one of the Scripps newspapers, a chain of afternoon dailies which covers the United States pretty thoroughly. You will note that a number of news stories which the Scripps paper had already published were reproduced along with the instructions in order that the correspondent might understand exactly what was wanted:

We reproduce several news items which recently appeared in this paper and they are samples of the sort of news our readers want.

It is suggested to correspondents that they read these articles carefully and see if they can recognize their stories.

Correspondents who follow the style of the stories submitted will find it easy to get their news printed in this paper.

We recently sent out circular letters for the purpose of revising the list of correspondents. Many new names appear

on our lists as a result. Many have asked questions concerning what we want in the way of news.

We will try to cover all the questions in a general way.

What we want:

News of general interest. News which will interest people in towns fifty miles from where you live. We cover northern and eastern Kentucky, West Virginia, southern Indiana, and southern Ohio. A news item from Jackson, O., should be of enough interest to be read by a reader in southern Indiana.

Murders always are of more than local interest.

Fires where damage is over $10,000 or where there is some unusual circumstances are interesting.

Missing girls make general news. So do unusual complaints in divorce cases, or unusual acts of dumb animals.

Remember this: Every news item should carry names with initials, place, age, and time. Never send an item reading: "Child of James Adams killed." Always give the name of the child, with its age, etc. Many items are thrown away because they are not complete.

If the item is a big one, use the telephone or telegraph, which ever will get it to us first. Every correspondent should take pride in being the first to give a news item to the public.

Send mail stories of any event which happens after 2 p. m. unless it would be worth an extra. Mail stories reaching us on the early morning trains are almost certain to be published.

Look for the odd things in all stories. If you are in

doubt about telegraphing a story send a query of 20 or 30 words, telling what the story is and asking if we want it.

Keep your stories brief. Give all the facts in the fewest possible words. Read your stories as they appear in print and you will see they have been cut to the bone. Write them that way and save yourself work, and still get just as much money for it.

We pay at the rate of one-half cent a word for matter used but often overpay a correspondent for special work.

A word about corellating reporting and correspondence:

As has been mentioned in an earlier lesson there are correspondents of many kinds, working in various ways. Some are paid by the column while others are on a salary: some represent county-seat papers, or others correspond for metropolitan publications, news associations, or trade papers.

There are also men and women who are professional correspondents, representing a string of papers in various parts of the country. In some instances they can put one story on the wire for all their papers, although such occasions are rare on account of the wide difference in news values in different localities. A story in which the central figure is a person of national repute would be worthy of use by the entire list of papers.

It is often the case that men and women correspondents who represent one or more newspapers outside their home towns have other employment at home, frequently on a newspaper. This, of course, keeps them in touch with local news at all times and makes their correspondence work comparatively simple, since they can then choose the

stories which will be of interest to their out-of-town newspapers without having to run around and gather facts.

If you are not connected with a local newspaper, get well acquainted with the editors and extend them courtesies whenever the opportunity arises. You will be given entree to their news and in all probability accorded a chance to read their proofs. What is even more to the point, you can interview their reporters who are fresh from a big story. Get on friendly terms with their best reporters and you will have a chance to accompany them on their assignments. This should not only prove instructive to you, giving you an insight into the methods of experienced men, but by working with different men you can get the various viewpoints. No two men see the same thing in the same light, and no two reporters write a story in the same manner, although both accounts may be perfectly clear, lucid and truthful.

Review Questions.

1. What are five general rules that must never be forgotten?
2. Who should the newspaper man cultivate as friends?
3. Of what value is the golden rule in the newspaper man's work?
4. What is meant by the correspondent's "string?"
5. Have you studied carefully the set of rules shown in this lesson? Study them again--they are important and they are in a general sense the rules laid down by every editor.

Lesson IV.

EXPRESSIONS TO AVOID.

A goodie may be "tasty." Decorations are "tasteful."

Don't say "he plead guilty." The past tense of "plead" is "pleaded."

Don't say "partially" for "partly.' "Partially" means with prejudice. A building is "partly" of brick.

Don't say "a man by (or "of") the name of Smith." Say "a man named Smith," or "Smith" or "one Smith."

Don't say "the then governor." "Then" is an adverb.

Don't begin a sentence with numerals. Spell out, or recast the sentence.

"Whereabouts" and "politics" are singular nouns.

Don't say "in our midst."

Don't use "inaugurate" for "begin." A movement is "begun;" a president is "inaugurated."

Use simple diction; and never use technical terms that are not generally understood, or words or phrases that are known as "fine" writing."

Don't abbreviate names, as "Geo." for "George," "Jno." for "John," etc. And endeavor to write the name of a person (particularly if well-known) as he or she is accustomed to write it. For example, "William Jennings Bryan," not "W. J. Bryan." "Elihu Root," not "E. Root."

Don't use "don't" when you mean "doesn't."

Don't say "he walked a distance of a mile." Omit "a distance of."

Don't begin your story with a general statement such as "A terrible accident occurred last night." Tell what really happened.

Don't try to save money for the office by crowding your copy on a sheet without margins. Leave plenty of white space at the top and bottom so the sheets can be pasted together.

Don't speak of a climate as "healthy." Persons are "healthy," places "healthful." A reporter once was considered very amusing when he asked a zoologist: "Are oysters healthy?" The answer was: "I never heard one complain."

Don't confuse "occur" with "take place." Things occur accidentally or by chance, while they take place by pre-arrangement.

Don't "sustain" broken legs and other injuries.

Don't "administer" punishment.

Don't say "among those present were----and others." Leave out "and others."

Don't tell the reader "this is a pathetic story." If it is, he will find it out for himself.

Don't overwork "well-known" and "prominent."

Don't say "Jones was present at the meeting and spoke." Of course, he was present. Simply say he "spoke."

Don't call a dog a "canine." "Canine" is an adjective.

Don't call a body found in a stream a "floater" or a "stiff." Never say, a body was "shipped"-- use "sent."

Don't speak of "Broadway st."--"Broadway" is enough.

Don't say "an old man 80 years of age." It's sufficient to say that he is "80 years old."

Don't say "5 o'clock p. m. yesterday afternoon." Say either

"5 p. m. yesterday" or "5 o'clock yesterday afternoon," according to the style of your paper.

Don't write "at an early hour this morning," when "early this morning" will do.

Don't write "at about." Usually, "about" will suffice.

Don't write "midnight yesterday" or "midnight last night." "Last midnight" is preferred.

Don't say "completely destroyed." "Destroyed" is sufficient.

Don't say "the money was divided between Smith, Jones and Brown." It was divided "among" them. Use "between" in reference to two only.

Don't confuse "perspicacity" and "perspicuity." Or "farther" and "further."

Don't confuse "quantity" and "amount."

Don't use "less" and "fewer" interchangeably.

Never start a story with "there."

Avoid such words as "however" and "very." Be sparing in the use of superlatives.

Be consistent in the use of collective nouns and their corresponding pronouns. If you speak of the audience as "its," continue the singular and do not refer later on to "their."

There is no such word as "enthuse."

Don't say "at the present time." Say "at present" or "now."

Don't write "cold in death." "Dead" will answer.

Don't confound "audiences," "spectators," and casual "witnesses."

Don't say "party" for "person."

Don't use "suicide," "loan," or "scare" as verbs.

Don't use "gotten;" it is questionable; use "got."

Don't use "burglarize."

Don't use "transpire" for "occur."

Don't use "locate" for "find;" to "locate" a thing is to place it.

Don't use "stopped" for "stayed;" he "stayed at the Central Hotel."

Don't "tender" receptions nor "render" songs; use "give" and "sing."

Don't "put in an appearance;" just "appear."

Don't use "stated" for "said."

Don't say "per day" or "per year," but "a day," "a year;" per is a Latin word and can be used only before a Latin noun, as "per diem" or "per annum."

Don't say "the meeting convened;" members might "convene" but a single body cannot.

Don't "claim that" anything is so; you can "claim" a thing, however.

Don't say "Mrs. Dr. Smith," just "Mrs. Smith."

Don't say "between" when more than two are mentioned.

Don't use "proven" for "proved."

Don't confound "staid" with "stayed."

Don't say "different than," but "different from."

Don't split infinitives or other verbs.

Don't use "onto."

Don't use "babe" or "tot" for "baby" or "child."

Don't use superlatives when you can help it.

Don't use trite expressions or foreign words and phrases.

Don't use "corner of" in designating street location.

Don't say "died from operation," but "died after operation"--to avoid danger of libel.

Don't get the "very" habit.

Don't use "couple of" instead of "two."

Don't use "Mr." before a man's full name.

Don't use slang unless it is fitting--which is seldom.

Don't mention the reporters, singly or collectively, unless it is necessary. It rarely is.

Don't qualify the word "unique;" a thing may be "unique," but it cannot be "very unique," "quite unique," "rather unique," or "more unique."

Don't use the inverted passive: e. g., "A man was given a dinner," "Smith was awarded a medal."

Don't concoct long and improper titles: Justice of the Supreme Court Smith, Superintendent of the Insurance Department Jones, Groceryman Brown. If the title is long put it after the man's name; thus: George Smith, justice of the Supreme Court.

Don't use the verb "occur" with weddings, receptions, etc.; they take place by design and never unexpectedly.

Don't say "a member of," if you can help it. Be specific.

Don't use the word "lady" for "woman," or "gentleman" for "man."

Don't use "depot" for "station"--railway passenger station.

Following is a list of bromides--trite, overworked expressions--that should be avoided:

conventional black
breakneck speed
durance vile
beautiful and accomplished
bonds of matrimony
burly negro
caught like a rat in a trap
Dan Cupid
Oil King (for "Rockefeller")
clutches of the law
long arm of justice
checkered career
demure miss
devouring element
towering giant
sickening thud
near death's door
failed to materialize
fiery steed
grim reaper
sickening sight
great beyond
grand old party
heartrending screams
knights of the grip
launched into eternity
last sad rites
minions of the law
tell it to the Marines
nipped in the bud
police character
weak as a cat
present incumbent
well-known club man
the pace that kills
viewed the remains
vanished as if the earth had swallowed him up
united in the bonds of matrimony
unfortunate victim
under cover of the darkness
totally destroyed
succulent bivalve
knee deep in June
petrified with fear
spread like wildfire
silver-toned orator
serious but not necessarily fatal
scene beggared description
rising young lawyer (or business man, physician, etc.)
severed all connections
fortune smiled on him

Review Questions.

1. Don't be afraid to study this lesson over and over again--the habit of using old and trite expressions just because they are easy to write and quickly thought of has spoiled the chances of many correspondents.

Lesson X.

BRANCHES OF CORRESPONDENCE.

In the foregoing lessons various branches of newspaper correspondence are set out, explaining roughly the qualifications necessary to carry on the work. There are other conditions, however, which affect the prospective correspondent, and which should be considered in determining the line of work to be pursued. First, experience in newspaper reportorial work is not only useful but almost essential in shaping a successful career in journalism. Now, where can this experience be obtained in the shortest possible time? Obviously on the staff of a metropolitan daily or the staff of a daily paper in a fair-size town. But daily papers almost without exception refuse to accept men without previous experience in reporting, even where these men are college graduates. This apparently leaves but one avenue open--the small-town daily or weekly newspaper. Again, there is an advantage in this condition because, while working as a reporter on a county-seat daily or weekly newspaper you can also act as correspondent for a newspaper in a large city, or for a big press association, thus gaining experience as correspondent while learning the duties of a newspaper reporter.

It is not so far a cry as it might seem from country correspondent and reporter to the staff of a big-city daily. Experience in the work, even in a small country town, breeds confidence in your own ability and fitness for bigger things. It is not difficult to see, from a purely commercial standpoint, that reporting and correspondence in a small country town would not yield large returns,

although a living could be made by representing a large list of papers as correspondent while working as reporter for your local weekly. If, for example, you lived in Germantown, Ohio, you might act as correspondent for Dayton newspapers, a newspaper in Columbus, (the state capital,) and a number of country weeklies in surrounding counties. It will be seen, however, that the scarcity of important happenings--stories of sufficient merit to interest people in larger towns and cities--would greatly curtail your earnings. The aim, then, is to gain sufficient experience in the country town to be capable of undertaking correspondence work in in a city, or reportorial work on the staff of a large-town daily daily paper.

Second in importance in its bearing on the prospective correspondent's career is his location. We have noted the limitations which residence in a country town places on a correspondent's earnings in considering ways and means for gaining experience. Let us now take up the case of one located in a fair-size town, say of 25,000 to 35,000; Newark, Ohio, for example. A man or woman located in Newark could act as correspondent for newspapers in Columbus, Cincinnati, Cleveland, and other big cities in Ohio; he could gather news for one of the big press associations, and might at the same time work on one of the local dailies. As Newark, Ohio, happens to be a glass and pottery manufacturing center, one could also correspond with trade papers covering these particular industries, especially if he were familiar with these trades. As a general rule, reporters working on daily papers in towns of this size have an abundance of time for other work. It then becomes a question as to which branch of correspondence work will best advance you financially as well as professionally.

Being near Columbus, the first and most desirable move would be to call on the state editor of one of the big papers in the capital city and arrange to act as correspondent in Newark. Each Columbus paper has many readers in Newark and a number of subscribers in surrounding smaller towns who are interested in events which take place in the smaller city, as well as numbers of Columbus readers whose business and social affiliations with Newark give importance to Newark happenings. You might find that between your reportorial work and correspondence with a Columbus paper your time would be pretty well taken up. If so, it would be better to handle these two situations creditably than to neglect them by undertaking additional duties. Again, you may learn that the Columbus papers are already represented in Newark by correspondents.

You should then write to the state editors of large-city papers throughout the state, such as Cleveland, Cincinnati, Toledo, Akron, Dayton, and Youngstown, offering to act as correspondent in Newark. In this instance you could act as correspondent for quite a list of papers, since substantially the same stories might be put on the wire for all. Your work too, would be limited to stories of state-wide or national importance, or local events of such extraordinary importance as would draw attention anywhere. In addition to this, you could act as correspondent for the Associated Press or United Press, because--aside from purely state news--your stories to large-city papers in the state could also be wired to the association.

The situation of the prospective correspondent in cities of 150,000 to 200,000, such as Dayton or Akron, Ohio, is little different

than in a town the size of Newark. The papers, being larger, may be a bit more exacting in their requirements as to the previous experience of persons seeking employment as reporters; but as a rule if you have shown marked ability in handling stories in a small town, you can at least get an opportunity to demonstrate your worth in the city. Taking Akron, Ohio, for example, you could act as correspondent for a paper in the capital and for publications in other large cities throughout the state--particularly Cleveland, which is only a few miles away--while working as reporter on an Akron daily. It is well to note, however, that the larger the city in which you are working, the less leisure will probably be left you for outside work. If you found a place on the staff of an Akron paper, therefore you would, no doubt, be confined to your reportorial work and

(a) representing a press association, or

(b) a few newspapers in large cities of the state, or

(c) a list of trade papers covering the tire and rubber trade, or

(d) a few newspapers in nearby smaller towns.

Your conditions would be very different if you elected to work as a correspondent only, in which case you might at one and the same time

(a) represent a press association, and

(b) a list of state newspapers not served by the association, and

(c) a list of trade papers, or nearby smaller-town dailies.

Many men, and women also, make good livings as correspondents, representing lists of newspapers and trade magazines. The number of papers and magazines served depends to a large extent on the ability

of the correspondent as understood by the publications, the speed with which he is able to cover a story, and last--but by no means least--his acquaintance with people who can put him in touch with stories which he can use. The correspondent who is not in the employ of a local newspaper must keep on friendly terms with one or more of the papers in his city so he can interview reporters fresh from a story or read proofs of the stories as set up for publication. This entails a willingness to do favors in return for courtesies extended, as well as the exercise of tact. No one can blame you for trying to secure the best stories for your list of papers, but use sufficient judgment in doing it, so as not to discommode those who are helping you.

Metropolitan centers afford larger opportunities alike for reporters and correspondents, but amid the hustle and bustle of such cities there is little room for a combination of the two professions. If you secured a place on the staff of a Cleveland, Ohio, daily as reporter, you would have little time to devote to correspondence work. It will also be seen that an engagement to cover Cleveland for a list of big-city newspapers, or a press syndicate, would not permit such a division of interest. Acting purely as a correspondent, however, you might find time to represent a large list of newspapers and one or two trade journals, or a press association and a few trade papers. One thing is certain: correspondents of more than average ability, energy and ambition are mighty well paid for their work in big cities, and the extent of their earnings need only be limited to the number of publications they are able to supply.

Review Questions.

1. Of what use is reportorial experience to the journalist?
2. How can such experience be gained? Do the country town papers offer a chance to gain it?
3. How would you go about getting the assignment as local correspondent for a list of papers?
4. What is there to gain in representing a trade paper?
5. How does the correspondent keep in touch with the happenings that might furnish him with stories?

Lesson XI.

CORRESPONDENCE AS A BREAD WINNER; THE TRADES.

A large percentage of the public erroneously regards correspondence work in the light of a side line; a profession that brings only "pin money" to those who practice it. It is only necessary to cite the case of the late Richard Harding Davis to dispel such misconceptions. The man (or woman) who is willing to devote his best efforts to perfecting himself as a harvester and writer of news is certain of ample reward in fame and cash. And what more is offered by any other line of endeavor? It is true that only a limited number ever attain the prominence of a Davis or a McClure, but today there are thousands of men and women who make handsome incomes in various phases of correspondence work.

Some of these people act as professional correspondents, devoting their entire working hours to the gathering of news for a number of newspapers, trade papers or magazines. Others, who are employed either as reporters or in some other capacity on a newspaper, where they have some leisure, work as correspondents in a more restricted way, but generally with a view to enlarging the scope of their work at some future time. They all regard their work seriously and strive for some particular objective. One man or woman wishes to be a feature writer; another desires to become a theatrical critic, and still another wants to star as a sport writer. Most persons do best the work they love, which explains why a great many correspondents see their ambitious dreams materialize. Editors are quick to note exceptional talent in a writer, and sooner or later the hard

worker is given his big chance. Witness the struggle and rise of Thornton W. Burgess, creator of the "Bedtime Stories," and the spectacular advance of H. C. Witwer, author of a hundred humorous short stories. What these men did, others can do with their own particular talents, and although there are difficulties to be overcome rich rewards await those strong enough to brave them. Burgess did not shine as a newspaper man. He wrote the now famous Bedtime Stories first for the amusement of his own children, totally unaware of their interest to thousands of other youngsters all over the land. His wife's persistent requests and his urgent need for money finally caused him to send one of these stories to a newspaper and resulted in their adoption by papers in every part of the United States.

TRADE PAPERS AND MAGAZINES.

Trade papers and magazines occupy a field separate and distinct from that of newspapers, although ability to write accurately and entertainingly is just as necessary. As a matter of fact, it requires considerable skill to set out a purely technical subject in an interesting manner, and a goodly part of trade-paper correspondence has to do with the technical.

To act as a trade-paper or magazine correspondent you must be located in a town sufficiently large to be considered a trade center. For example, Newark and Zanesville, Ohio, are pottery centers; Pittsburgh, Pa., Cleveland and Youngstown, Ohio, are iron and steel centers, while St. Louis, Mo., Boston, Mass., and Cincinnati, Ohio, are shoe and leather trade headquarters. In addition to this, you must have intimate knowledge of the trade about which you are going to write. It is obviously impossible for a man who knows nothing

about the processes of making steel rails to write intelligently on the subject, and his unfamiliarity with the subject would be immediately apparent to readers of the paper.

The trade-paper field, however, covers almost every industry and profession. Thus a young physician in a town large enough to boast one or more big hospitals might well act as correspondent for several medical magazines; a musician in any city having a variety of high-class musical organizations could profitably write for "The Etude" and other musical publications, and an automobile salesman or mechanic in a motor car manufacturing center could make money covering the trade for a list of motor journals.

It is necessary, right at the start, that the prospective correspondent understand that in the trade-paper field the "shoemaker must cleave to his last." Of course, a man or woman may well be experienced in a trade and at the same time possess talent in one or more of the arts or professions. In such cases one could cover two fields, but in most instances it is better to attempt to write first only on the subject which you understand best. Thus, if you make a business of building motor boats and play a musical instrument only in your leisure hours, by all means cover the motor-boat industry rather than music. Never under any circumstances attempt to write on a subject where you are not sure of your ground. Better write less than attempt to earn more by "stalling."

Here is a list of trade papers and their addresses. To establish relations as correspondent, write to the editors of the papers covering your particular trade, profession or art:

ADVERTISING

Advertising and Selling	New York City
Advertising World	Columbus, Ohio
Associated Advertising	New York City
Class	Chicago, Ill.
Editor and Publisher	New York City
Fourth Estate	New York City
Mailbag, The	Cleveland, Ohio
Newspaperdom	New York City
Pollock's Newspaper News	Minneapolis, Minn.
Postage	New York City
Poster, The	Chicago, Ill.
Printers' Ink	New York City
Printers' Ink Monthly	New York City
Signs of The Times	Cincinnati, Ohio
Western Advertising	San Francisco, Calif.

AERONAUTIC

Ace, The	Los Angeles, Calif.
Aerial Ace	New York City
Air Power	New York City
Aviation and Aircraft Journal	New York City
Flying	New York City
U. S. Air Service	Washington, D. C.

ARCHITECTURE

American Architect	New York City
Architect's Buyers Reference	New York City
Architect and Engineer	San Francisco, Calif.

Architecture	New York City
Architecture and Building	New York City
Architectural Forum	Boston, Mass.
Architectural Record	New York City
Architectural Review	New York City
Building Review	San Francisco, Calif.
Journal of American Institute of Architects	New York City
Modern Building	Detroit, Mich.
Pencil Points	New York City
Sweet's Architectural Catalogue	New York City
Western Architect	Chicago, Ill.

ART

Art and Archaeology	Washington, D. C.
National Art Student	New York City

AUTOMOBILE, GAS ENGINES, ETC.

Accessory and Garage Journal	Pawtucket, R. I.
American Automobile Digest	Cincinnati, Ohio
American Garage and Auto Dealer	Chicago, Ill.
Automobile Blue Book	New York City
Auto Dealer and Repairer	New York City
Auto Review	St. Louis, Mo.
Automobile Builder	Cleveland, Ohio
Automobile Journal	Pawtucket, R. I.
Automobile Topics	New York City
Automobile Trade Directory	New York City
Automobile Trade Journal	Philadelphia, Pa.

Automobilist	Boston, Mass.
Automotive Electrical Engineer	Chicago, Ill.
Automotive Industries	New York City
Automotive Manufacturer	New York City
Buffalo Motorist	Buffalo, N. Y.
California Ford Owner	Los Angeles, Calif.
Chilton Automobile Directory	Philadelphia, Pa.
Commercial Car Journal	Philadelphia, Pa.
Commercial Vehicle	New York City
Dixie Motor News	Atlanta, Ga.
Ford Car Trade Journal	Chicago, Ill.
Ford News	Long Island, N. Y.
Ford Owner and Dealer	Milwaukee, Wis.
Ford Trade Directory	Long Island City, N. Y.
Garage Dealer	Minneapolis, Minn.
Gas	Milwaukee, Wis.
Highway Transportation	New York City
Honk-Honk	Cincinnati, Ohio
Hoosier Motorist	Indianapolis, Ind.
Journal of Society of Automotive Engineers	New York City
Maryland Motorist	Baltimore, Md.
Massachusetts Auto List & Tourist	Boston, Mass.
Motor	New York City
Motor Age	Chicago, Ill.
Motor Guide	Rochester, Ind.
Motorist, The	Omaha, Neb.

Motor Record	New York City
Motor Service	Chicago, Ill.
Motor Travel	New York City
Motor Truck	Pawtucket, R. I.
Motor West	Los Angeles, Calif.
Motor World	New York City
New Jersey Automobile Journal	Red Bank, N. J.
New Jersey Motorist	New Brunswick, N. J.
Northwest Motorist and Truckman	Seattle, Wash.
Pacific Golf and Motor	San Francisco, Calif.
Power Wagon	Chicago, Ill.
Power Wagon Reference Book	Chicago, Ill.
Southern Automotive Dealer	Atlanta, Ga.
Southern Motorist	New Orleans, La.
Speed	Wilmington, Del.
Steering Wheel	Dallas, Texas
Tib Automobile Route Books	Kansas City, Mo.
Tire Rate Book	Kansas City, Mo.
Tire Rate Book	New York City
Tire Trade Journal and Vulcanizer and Tire Dealer	New York City
Tires	New York City
Touring Topics	Los Angeles, Calif.
Truck Owner	Philadelphia, Pa.
Vehicle Monthly	Philadelphia, Pa.
Virginia-Carolina Motorist	Richmond, Va.
Western Motor	Denver, Col.
Wisconsin Motorist	Milwaukee, Wis.

BAKING

Bakers' Helper	Chicago, Ill.
Baker's News	Chicago, Ill.
Baker's Review	New York City
Bakers' Weekly	New York City
Cracker Baker	New York City
National Baker	Philadelphia, Pa.
New South Baker	Atlanta, Ga.
Pacific Bakery World	Los Angeles, Calif.
Retail Baker	Brooklyn N Y
Western Baker	San Francisco, Calif.

BARRELS, BOXES AND PACKAGES

American Box Maker	Chicago, Ill.
Barrel and Box, The	Chicago, Ill.
Carton Age	Chicago, Ill.
Fibre Containers	Chicago, Ill.
Package Advertiser	Chicago, Ill.
Shears	Lafayette, Ind.

BLACKSMITH AND HORSE SHOERS

American Blacksmith, Auto and Tractor Shop	Buffalo, N. Y.
Blacksmith and Wheelwright	New York City

BOOKS, BOOK TRADE AND WRITERS

Books of the Month	New York City
Book Review	New York City
Dial, The	New York City
Library Journal	New York City

Public Libraries	Chicago, Ill.
Publishers' Weekly	New York City
Wilson Trio	New York City
Writer's Digest, The	Cincinnati, Ohio

BOTTLING

American Bottler	New York City
Beverage Journal	Chicago, Ill.
Beverage News	New York City
Coca Cola Bottler, The	Hickory, N. C.
National Bottlers' Gazette	New York City
Pacific Bottler	San Francisco, Calif.
Southern Carbonator and Bottler	Atlanta, Ga.

BRICK, TILE, ETC.

Brick and Clay Record	Chicago, Ill.
Clay Worker	Indianapolis, Ind.

BUILDING AND BUILDING MATERIALS

American Builder	Chicago, Ill.
American Building Association News	Cincinnati, Ohio
American Contractor	Chicago, Ill.
American Roofer	Chicago, Ill.
Builder's Guide	Philadelphia, Pa.
Builder's Journal	Boston, Mass.
Builders' Weekly Guide	Baltimore, Md.
Building Age	New York City
Building and Engineering Digest	Dallas, Texas
Building and Engineering News	San Francisco, Calif.
Building Industry	Cleveland, Ohio

Building Materials	Detroit, Mich.
Building Supply News	Chicago, Ill.
Building Witness	Cincinnati, Ohio
Carpenter, The	New York City
Improvement Bulletin	Minneapolis, Minn.
Kansas Construction News	Topeka, Kansas
National Builder	Chicago, Ill.
Oklahoma Construction News	Topeka, Kansas
Pacific Builder and Engineer	Seattle, Wash.
Permanent Builder, The	Chicago, Ill.
Southern Architect and Building News	Atlanta, Ga.
Southern Construction News	Little Rock, Ark.
Southwest Builder and Contractor	Los Angeles, Calif.
Western Builder	Milwaukee, Wis.
Western Contractor	Kansas City, Mo.

BUILDING MANAGEMENT

Buildings and Building Management	Chicago, Ill.

BUSINESS AND OFFICE METHODS

Administration	New York City
American Business National Acceptance Journal	New York City
Bookkeeper and Accountant	St. Louis, Mo.
Business	Detroit, Mich.
Business Philosopher	Memphis, Tenn.
Gregg Writer	Chicago, Ill.
Journal of Accountancy	New York City
Lefax	Philadelphia, Pa.

Lefax Catalog Data Sheets	Philadelphia, Pa.
Sabean, The	New York City
Sales Management	Chicago, Ill.
Sales Manager	New York City
Silent Partner	New York City

BUTCHERS AND MEAT PACKERS

Butchers' Advocate	New York City
National Provisioner	Chicago, Ill.

CANNING, DRYING AND PRESERVING

Canner, The	Chicago, Ill
Canning Age	New York City
Canning Trade, The	Baltimore, Md.
Evaporator, The	Webster, N. Y.
Western Canner and Packer	San Francisco, Calif.

CARRIAGES AND HARNESS

Harness	New York City
Harness Dealer, The	Des Moines, Ia.
Harness Gazette	Rome, N. Y.
Harness Herald	Chicago, Ill
Harness World	Cincinnati, Ohio
Spokesman, The	Cincinnati, Ohio

CEMENT AND CONCRETE

Cement and Engineering News	Chicago, Ill
Cement, Mill and Quarry	Chicago, Ill
Concrete	Detroit, Mich.
Concrete (Mill Edition)	Detroit, Mich.
Concrete Age	Atlanta, Ga.
Concrete Products	Chicago, Ill.
Western Cement and Concrete	San Francisco, Calif.

CEMETERY AND MONUMENTS

Granite, Marble and Bronze	Boston, Mass.
Monument and Cemetery Review	Buffalo, N. Y.
Monumental News	Chicago, Ill.
Park and Cemetery	Chicago, Ill.

CHEMICALS, CHEMISTRY AND COLOR

American Dyestuff Reporter	New York City
Annual Chemical Directory	Baltimore, Md.
Chemical Age	New York City
Chemical, Color and Oil Daily	New York City
Chemical and Metallurgical Engineering	New York City
Chemical Engineering Catalog	New York City
Color Trade Journal	New York City
Drug and Chemical Markets	New York City
Journal of Biological Chemistry	Baltimore, Md.
Journal of Industrial and Engineering Chemistry	New York City

CLEANING AND DYEING

Cleaners and Dyer's Review	Cincinnati, Ohio
Cleaning and Dyeing World	Chicago, Ill.
National Cleaner and Dyer	Chicago, Ill.

CLOTHING AND FURNISHING GOODS (Men's)

American Gentlemen	New York City
American Hatter	New York City
Boys' Outfitter	New York City
Chicago Apparel Gazette	Chicago, Ill.
Clothier and Furnisher	New York City
Clothing Trade Journal	New York City

Fairchild's Directories	New York City
National Directory and Digest	New York City
Haberdasher, The	New York City
International Tailor	New York City
Manufacturing Clothier	New York City
Men's Wear	Chicago, Ill.
National Clothier	Chicago, Ill.
Progressive Tailor	New York City
Sartorial Art Journal	New York City
Shirt and Undergarment Trade Journal	New York City

CLOTHING (Women's)

American Cloak and Suit Review	New York City
Costumes and Dresses	New York City
Daily Garment News	New York City
Fairchild's Directories	New York City
National Directory Digest	New York City
Garment Manufacturers' Index	New York City
National Garment Retailer	New York City
Nugent's--The Garment Weekly	New York City
Women's Wear	New York City

COAL, COKE, ETC.

American Coal Journal	New York City
American Coal Miner	Indianapolis, Ind.
Black Diamond	Chicago, Ill.
Coal Age	New York City
Coal Catalog	Pittsburgh, Pa.
Coal Dealer, The	Minneapolis, Minn.

Coal Industry	Pittsburgh, Pa.
Coal Mining Review	Columbus, Ohio
Coal Review	Washington, D. C.
Coal Trade Bulletin	Pittsburgh, Pa.
Coal Trade Journal	New York City
Mining Catalogue	Pittsburgh, Pa.
Retail Coalman, The	Chicago, Ill.
Saward's Journal	New York City

COMMERCIAL (General)

American Industries	New York City
Annalist	New York City
Board of Trade Journal	Scranton, Pa.
Bulletin of Commerce	St. Louis, Mo.
Business Digest Service	New York City
Chicago Commerce	Chicago, Ill.
Commercial Index	Salt Lake City, Utah
Commercial News and Labor Gazette	St. Louis, Mo.
Commercial Record	New Haven, Conn.
Current Affairs	Boston, Mass.
Daily News Record	New York City
Hendricks Commercial Register of the United States	New York City
Journal of Commerce	Philadelphia, Pa.
Mercantile Adjuster	St. Louis, Mo.
Mich. Mfgr. and Financial Record	Detroit, Mich.
Ohio Journal of Commerce	Columbus, Ohio
Philadelphia C. of C. News Bulletin	Philadelphia, Pa.
Public Service Journal	San Francisco, Calif.
Thomas' Register of Am. Mfgrs.	New York City

COMMERCIAL TRAVELERS

Commercial Traveler's Magazine	Springfield, Mass.
National Commercial Traveler	New Orleans, La.
Pacific Coast Commercial Traveler	San Francisco, Calif.
Sample Case	Columbus, Ohio
T. P. A. Magazine	St. Louis, Mo.

CONFECTIONERY, ICE CREAM AND SODA FOUNTAIN

Candy and Ice Cream	Chicago, Ill.
Candy and Soda Profits	St. Paul, Minn.
Candy Factory	Chicago, Ill.
Candy Jobber	Chicago, Ill.
Candy Manufacturer	Chicago, Ill.
Confectionery Merchandising	Chicago, Ill.
Confectioners' Gazette	New York City
Confectioners' Journal	Philadelphia, Pa.
Confectioners' Review	Cincinnati, Ohio
Fountain Profits	Portland, Oregon
Ice Cream Review	Milwaukee, Wis.
Ice Cream Trade Journal	New York City
International Confectioner	New York City
Northwest Soft Drink and Candy Journal	Minneapolis, Minn.
Northwestern Confectioner	Milwaukee, Wis.
Soda Dispenser	Atlanta, Ga.
Soda Fountain	New York City
Soft Drink Journal	New York City
Sweets	Atlanta, Ga.
Western Confectioner	San Francisco, Calif.

CONTRACTING, EXCAVATION, ETC.

Bulletin of Associated Gen. Contractors	Washington, D. C.
Contractors and Engineers' Monthly	New York City
Earth Mover	Aurora, Ill.
Excavating Engineer	South Milwaukee, Wis.
Mich. Contractor and Builder	Detroit, Mich.
Roadmaker, Excavator and Grader	Chicago, Ill.
Steam Shovel and Dredge	Chicago, Ill.

DENTAL.

American Dentist	Chicago, Ill.
Chicago Dental Soc'y Official Bulletin	Chicago, Ill.
Dental Cosmos	Philadelphia, Pa.
Dental Digest	New York City
Dental Facts	Chicago, Ill.
Dental Items of Interest	Brooklyn, N. Y.
Dental Outlook	New York City
Dental Summary	Toledo, Ohio
Journal of National Dental Ass'n.	Chicago, Ill.
Oral Hygiene	Pittsburgh, Pa.
Pacific Dental Gazette	San Francisco, Calif.
Practical Dental Journal	San Antonio, Texas
Texas Dental Journal	Dallas, Texas

DRAMATIC AND THEATRICAL

Billboard, The	Cincinnati, Ohio
Boston Times, The	Boston, Mass.
Drama, The	Chicago, Ill.
Dramatic Mirror	New York City

Dramatic	Easton, Pa.
New York Clipper	New York City
New York Dramatic News	New York City
Opera House Reporter	Des Moines, Iowa.
Variety	New York City

DRUGS, PHARMACEUTIC, ETC.

American Druggist	New York City
American Journal of Pharmacy	Philadelphia, Pa.
American Registered Pharmacists' Journal	San Francisco, Calif.
Apothecary and New England Druggist	Boston, Mass.
Bulletin of Pharmacy	Detroit, Mich.
California Druggist	Los Angeles, Calif.
California Retail Drug Journal	Los Angeles, Calif.
C. R. D. A. News	Chicago, Ill.
Drugdom	Chicago, Ill.
Drug Store Merchandising	Chicago, Ill.
Drug Topics	New York City
Drug Trade Weekly	New York City
Druggist, The	Memphis, Tenn.
Druggist Circular, The	New York City
Journal of American Pharmaceutical Association	Philadelphia, Pa.
Kentucky Druggist	Louisville, Ky.
Meyer Druggist	St. Louis, Mo.
Modern Druggist	New Orleans, La.
N. A. R. D. Journal	Chicago, Ill.
National Druggist	St. Louis, Mo.

Northwestern Druggist	St. Paul, Minn.
Oil, Paint and Drug Reporter	New York, N. Y.
P. A. R. D. Bulletin	Philadelphia, Pa.
Pacific Drug Review	Portland, Ore.
Pharmaceutical Era, The	New York City
Practical Druggist	New York City
Proprietary Record	Atlanta, Ga.
Retail Druggist	Detroit, Mich.
Rocky Mountain Druggist	Denver, Col.
Southern Pharmaceutical Journal	Dallas, Texas
Spatula	Boston, Mass.
Standard Remedies	Chicago, Ill.
Stirring Rod, The	San Francisco, Calif.
Voice, The	Long Island, N. Y.
Western Druggist	Chicago, Ill.

DRY GOODS

Apparel Criterion	Seattle, Wash.
Atlantic Coast Merchant	New York City
Corsets and Lingerie	New York City
Corset and Underwear Review	New York City
Dress Essentials	New York City
Dry Goods	New York City
Dry Goods Economist	New York City
Dry Goods Merchants' Trade Journal	Des Moines, Iowa
Dry Goods Reporter	Chicago, Ill.
Drygoodsman	St. Louis, Mo.
Economist Group, The	New York City

Lace and Embroidery Review	New York City
Pacific Coast Merchant	San Francisco, Calif.
Southeastern Dry Goods Merchant	Atlanta, Ga.
Southern Merchant	Atlanta, Ga.
Sweater News and Knitted Outerwear	New York City
Underwear and Hosiery Review	New York City

EDUCATIONAL

American School Board Journal	Milwaukee, Wis.
Business Educator	Columbus, Ohio
Illinois Teacher and School and Home Education	Bloomington, Ill.
Industrial Arts Mag.	Milwaukee, Wis.
Kansas Teacher and Western School Journal	Topeka, Kansas
Manual Training Magazine	Peoria, Ill.
National School Digest	New York City
Progressive Teacher	Morristown, Tenn.
School and Home Education	Bloomington, Ill.
School and Society	New York City
Science	New York City
Scientific Monthly	New York City

ELECTRICAL

Central Station, The	New York City
EMF Electrical Year Book	Chicago, Ill.
Electrical Journal	Pittsburgh, Pa.
Electrical Contractor-Dealer	New York City
Electrical Merchandising	New York City
Electrical Record	New York City

Electrical Review	Chicago, Ill.
Electrical South	Atlanta, Ga.
Electrical World	New York City
General Electrical Review	Schenectady, N. Y.
Jobber's Salesman	Chicago, Ill.
Journal of Am. Inst. Electrical Engineers	New York City
Journal of Electricity and Western Industry	San Francisco, Calif.
Public Service Management	Chicago, Ill.

ENGINEERING

Engineering and Contracting	Chicago, Ill.
Engineering News Record	New York City
Engineering World	Chicago, Ill.
Iowa Engineer	Ames, Iowa
Journal of Engineering	Boulder, Col.
Professional Engineer	Chicago, Ill.
Sweet's Engineering Catalogue	New York City

EXPORT TRADE

American Directory and Buyer's Guide	New York City
American Exporter	New York City
Ante Ojos	New York City
Automotive Exporter	New York City
Cine Mundial	New York City
Commercial America	Philadelphia, Pa.
Cuba Review	New York, N. Y.
Dun's International Review	New York City
Edicion En Espanol	Chicago, Ill.

Edicion Pan-American	Philadelphia, Pa.
El Automovil Americano	New York City
El Automovilismo	New York City
El Campo.Internacional	New York City
El Comercio	New York City
El Ingeniero Y Contratista	New York City
El Mundo Azucarero	New Orleans, La.
El Reporter Latino Americano	Boston, Mass.
Electrical Export	New York City
El Norte Americano	New York City
Export American Industries	New York City
Export Trade and Exporters' Review	New York City
Exporters' and Importers' Journal	New York City
Exporters' Encyclopedia	New York City
Ferreteria	Atlanta, Ga.
Geyer's Revista International	New York City
Gulf Ports	New Orleans, La.
Importers' Guide	New York City
Ingenieria International	New York City
International Cinema Trade Review	New York City
International Trade Developer	Chicago, Ill.
Iron Age Catalogue of Am. Exports	New York City
Japanese-American Commercial Weekly	New York City
Kelly's Customs Tariffs of The World	New York City
Kelly's Dir. of Merchants, Mfgrs. and Shippers of the World	New York City

La America	New York City
La Hacienda	Buffalo, N. Y.
La Industria	New York City
La Revista Del Mundo	Garden City, N. Y.
Levant American Commercial Review	New York City
Mercurio	New Orleans, La.
Office Appliance Exporter	Chicago, Ill.
Pacific Ports	Seattle, Wash.
Pan Pacific Magazine	San Francisco, Calif.
Revista Americana	New York City
South American, The	New York City
South Atlantic Ports	Jacksonville, Fla.
Spanish Pictorial Review	New York City
Spanish Vogue	New York City
Weekly Export Bulletin	Philadelphia, Pa.
World's Markets, The	New York City

EXPRESS

Express Gazette Journal	New York City

FARM, IMPLEMENTS, TRACTORS, ETC.

Agrimotor	Chicago, Ill.
Chilton Tractor Index	Philadelphia, Pa.
Chilton Tractor Journal	Philadelphia, Pa.
Eastern Dealer in Implements and Vehicles	Philadelphia, Pa.
Farm Implements and Tractors	Minneapolis, Minn.
Farm Implement News	Chicago, Ill.
Farm-Light and Power	New York City
Farm Machinery and Farm Power	St. Louis, Mo.

Implement Hardware Bulletin	Abilene, Kansas
Imp. and Tractor Age	Springfield, Ohio
Implement and Tractor Trade Journal	Kansas City, Mo.
Implement Record	San Francisco, Calif.
N. W. Tractor and Truck Dealer	Minneapolis, Minn.
Power Farming Dealer	St. Joseph, Mich.
Tractor and Better Roads and Streets	Cincinnati, Ohio
Tractor and Gas Engine Review	Madison, Wis.
Tractor and Implement Blue Book	St. Louis, Mo.
Tractor Builder, The	Cleveland, Ohio
Tractor World	Pawtucket, R. I.

FASHION

American Ladies' Tailor	New York City
L'Elegance Parisienne	New York City
Les Parisiennes	New York City

FERTILIZER

American Fertilizer	Philadelphia, Pa.
Commercial Fertilizer	Atlanta, Ga.
Fertilizer Green Book	Chicago, Ill.

FINANCIAL AND BANKING

American Banker	New York City
American Globe	Los Angeles, Calif.
Banker-Manufacturer	Milwaukee, Wis.
Banker's Magazine	New York City
Banker's Monthly	Chicago, Ill.
Banker and Tradesman	Boston, Mass.
Banking Law Journal	New York City
Bond Buyer, The	New York City

Bond and Mortgages	Chicago, Ill.
Boston Commercial	Boston, Mass.
Burroughs' Clearing House	Detroit, Mich.
Business Chronicle of The Pacific Northwest	Seattle, Wash.
Central Banker of Chicago	Chicago, Ill.
Chicago Banker	Chicago, Ill.
Coast Banker	San Francisco, Calif.
Commerce and Finance	New York City
Commercial and Financial Chronicle	New York City
Commercial West	Minneapolis, Minn.
Credit Monthly	New York City
Credit World	St. Louis, Mo.
Daily Bond Buyer	New York City
Economist, The	Chicago, Ill.
Farm Loans and City Bonds	Chicago, Ill.
Finance and Industry	Cleveland, Ohio
Financial Age	New York City
Financial and Insurance News	Los Angeles, Calif.
Financial World, The	New York City
Financier, The	New York City
Journal of American Banker's Ass'n.	New York City
Kansas Banker	Topeka, Kansas
Lawyer and Banker	Detroit, Mich.
Magazine of Wall Street	New York City
Michigan Investor	Detroit, Mich.
Mid-Continent Banker	St. Louis, Mo.

Money and Commerce	Pittsburgh, Pa.
Montana Banker	Great Falls, Montana
Mountain States Banker	Denver, Col.
National Banker	Chicago, Ill.
N. A. Banker and Journal of Commerce	Chicago, Ill.
Northwestern Banker	Des Moines, Ia.
Ohio Banker	Columbus, Ohio
Southern Banker	Atlanta, Ga.
Southwestern Bankers' Journal	Oklahoma City, Okla.
Successful Banking	Benton Harbor, Mich.
Trans-Mississippi Banker	Kansas City, Mo.
United States Investor	Boston, Mass.
Western Banker	Omaha, Neb.
Western Financier	Kansas City, Mo.

FIRE, WATER AND POLICE

Fire and Water Engineering	New York City
Fire Engineer	New York City
Fire Protection	Indianapolis, Ind.
Fire Service	New York City
Fireman's Standard	Boston, Mass.
Journal of American Waterworks Association	New York City
Safety Engineering	New York City
State Trooper, The	Detroit, Mich.

FLORIST, FLORICULTURE AND PARKS

American Florist	Chicago, Ill.
Florists' Exchange	New York City
Florists' Review	Chicago, Ill.

Flower Grower, The	Calcium, N. Y.
Gardeners' Guide	New York City
Horticulture	Boston, Mass.
Park International	Washington, D. C.
Wisconsin Horticulture	Madison, Wis.

FOOD AND CULINARY

New Macaroni Journal	Braidwood, Ill.

FORESTRY

American Forestry	Washington, D. C.
Journal of Forestry	Washington, D. C.

FRUIT, POULTRY AND PRODUCE TRADE

Bean Bag, The	Lansing, Mich.
Egg Reporter, The	Waterloo, Ia.
Fruitman's Guide	New York City
Fruit Trade Journal and Produce Record	New York City
N. Y. Produce Rev. and Am. Creamery	New York City
Packer, The	Kansas City, Mo.
Produce Packer, The	Kansas City, Mo.
Peanut Promoter, The	Suffolk, Va.
Potato Magazine	Chicago, Ill.
Produce News, The	New York City
Strawberry Items	Chattanooga, Tenn.
Sweet Potato Bulletin	Mobile, Ala.
Western Fruit Jobber	Denver, Col.

FURNITURE, UPHOLSTERY AND CARPETS

American Carpet and Upholstery Journal	Philadelphia, Pa.
American Furniture Manufacturer	Chicago, Ill.

Carpet and Rug World	New York City
Carpet and Upholstery Trade Review	New York City
Decorative Furnisher	New York City
Decorative Furniture Directory and Buyer's Guide	New York City
Furniture Advertiser	Chicago, Ill.
Furniture Age	Chicago, Ill.
Furniture Dealer	Minneapolis, Minn.
Furniture Index	Jamestown, N. Y.
Furniture Journal	Chicago, Ill.
Furniture Mfgr. and Artisan	Grand Rapids, Mich.
Furniture Merchants' Trade Journal	Des Moines, Ia.
Furniture Record, Grand Rapids	Grand Rapids, Mich.
Furniture Trade Review	New York City
Furniture Worker	Cincinnati, Ohio
Furniture World	New York City
Good Furniture	Grand Rapids, Mich.
Pacific Furniture Trade	San Francisco, Calif.
Price's Carpet and Rug News	New York City
St. Louis Furniture News	St. Louis, Mo.
Southern Furniture Journal	High Point, N. C.
Upholster and Interior Decorator	New York City
Wall-Paper	New York City
Western Furniture	Portland, Oregon

FUR TRADE

American Albium of Fur Novelties	New York City
Black Fox Magazine	New York City
Fur Trade Review	New York City

GAS

Acetylene Journal	Chicago, Ill.
American Gas Journal	New York City
Gas Age	New York City
Gas Record	Chicago, Ill.
Natural Gas	Cincinnati, Ohio
Manufactured Gas Industry	Buffalo, N. Y.
Natural Gas Industry	Buffalo, N. Y.

GENERAL MERCHANDISE

Appalachian Trade Journal	Knoxville, Tenn.
Cincinnati Trade Review	Cincinnati, Ohio
Co-Operator, The	Chicago, Ill.
General Storekeeper	Waukegan, Ill.
General Store Marchandising	Chicago, Ill.
Heart O' Trade	Indianapolis, Ind.
Illinois Retail Merchants Journal	Peoria, Ill.
Inland Merchant	New York City
Little Rock Trade Record	Little Rock, Ark.
Los Angeles Apparel Gazette	Los Angeles, Calif.
Merchant, The	Dallas, Texas
Merchant's Index	Denver, Col.
Merchant's Journal	Topeka, Kansas
Merchant's Journal and Commerce	Richmond, Va.
Merchant and Manufacturer	Nashville, Tenn.
Michigan Tradesman	Grand Rapids, Mich.
Montana Trade Journal	Great Falls, Montana.
New West Trade	Spokane, Wash.

Northwest Commercial Bulletin	St. Paul, Minn.
Northwestern Merchant	Seattle, Wash.
Oregon Merchant's Magazine	Portland, Oregon
Pennsylvania Merchant	Philadelphia, Pa.
Price Current	Wichita, Kansas
Retail Selling	Oklahoma City, Okla.
Trade Exhibit	Omaha, Neb.
Trade Outlook, The	Louisville, Ky.
Variety Goods Magazine	Cincinnati, Ohio
Wholesale Grocery Review	New York City
Wisconsin Retail Merchants' Advo.	Fond du Lac, Wis.

GOOD ROADS

Good Roads	New York City
Highway Engineer and Contractor	Chicago, Ill.
Michigan Roads and Forests	Detroit, Mich.
Motor Highway	Lincoln, Nebr.
Pacific Street and Road Builder	San Francisco, Calif.
Southern Good Roads	Lexington, N. C.
Texas Oil News	San Marcos, Texas
Western Highway Builder	Los Angeles, Calif.

GROCERY

American Food Journal	New York City
American Grocer	New York City
Atlanta Retail Grocer	Atlanta, Ga.
Cincinnati Jobber and Retail Grocer	Cincinnati, Ohio
Commercial Bulletin	Los Angeles, Calif.
Denver Grocer	Denver, Col.

Duncan's Trade Register	Portland, Ore.
Facts and Figures	Jacksonville, Fla.
Grocer and Butcher	Toledo, Ohio
Grocer's Journal	Birmingham, Ala.
Grocers' Journal, The	Los Angeles, Calif.
Grocers' Magazine	Boston, Mass.
Grocers' Review	Philadelphia, Pa.
Indiana Grocer	Indianapolis, Ind.
Indiana Retail Grocers Bulletin	Indianapolis, Ind.
Interstate Grocer	St. Louis, Mo.
Kansas City Grocer	Kansas City, Mo.
Louisiana Grocer	New Orleans, La.
Modern Grocer	Chicago, Ill.
Modern Merchant and Grocery World	Philadelphia, Pa.
National Grocer	Chicago, Ill.
National Grocers' Bulletin	San Francisco, Calif.
New England Grocer and Tradesman	Boston, Mass.
New York Retail Grocers' Advocate	Brooklyn, N. Y.
Retail Grocers' Advocate	San Francisco, Calif.
Retailers' Journal	Chicago, Ill.
San Francisco Grocer	San Francisco, Calif.
Southeastern Grocer	Atlanta, Ga.
Spice Mill	New York City
Tacoma West Coast Trade	Tacoma, Wash.
Tea and Coffee Trade Journal	New York City
Wholesale Grocer	Chicago, Ill.

HARDWARE

American Artisan and Hardware Record	Chicago, Ill.
American Cutler	New York City
American Hardware Jobbers' Directory	Pittsburgh, Pa.
Good Hardware	New York City
Hardware Age	New York City
Hardware Age Directory of Am. Mfgrs.	New York City
Hardware Dealers' Magazine	New York City
Hardware Merchants' Trade Journal	Des Moines, Ia.
Hardware News	Pittsburgh, Pa.
Hardware Review	New York City
Hardware Salesman	Chicago, Ill.
Hardware Trade and Automobile News, The	St. Paul, Minn.
Hardware World	St. Louis, Mo.
Hardware and House Furnishing Goods	Atlanta, Ga.
Hardware and Implement Journal	Dallas, Texas
Merchandise Rating Register Hdwe.	New York City
National Hardware Bulletin	Argos, Ind.
New England Hardware News	Boston, Mass.
Pacific Hardware Journal	San Francisco, Calif.
Southern Hdwre. and Implement Jl.	Atlanta, Ga.

HOSPITALS, NURSING, ETC.

American Journal of Nursing	Rochester, N. Y.
Hospital Management	Chicago, Ill.
Hospital Progress	Milwaukee, Wis.
Modern Hospital	Chicago, Ill.

Modern Hospital Year Book	Chicago, Ill.
Pacific Coast Journal of Nursing	San Francisco, Calif.
Public Health Nurse, The	Cleveland, Ohio
Trained Nurse and Hospital Review	New York City

HOTEL, RESTAURANT, ETC.

American Restaurant	Chicago, Ill.
California Tourist and Hotel Reporter	Los Angeles, Calif.
Caterer and Hotel Prop. Gazette	New York City
Chef-Steward	Chicago, Ill.
Chilton Hotel Supply Index	Philadelphia, Pa.
Cross-Continent Hotel Trio	Chicago, Ill.
Delicatessen	New York City
Hotel and Club News	Philadelphia, Pa.
Hotel and Travel	Atlanta, Ga.
Hotel Bulletin	Chicago, Ill.
Hotel Gazette	New York City
Hotel Industry	New York City
Hotel Monthly	Chicago, Ill.
Hotel News of the West	Seattle, Wash.
Hotel Review	New York City
Hotel World	Chicago, Ill.
Keeler's Hotel Weekly	San Francisco, Calif.
Mid-West Hotel Reporter	Omaha, Neb.
National Restaurant News	Kansas City, Mo.
New York Hotel Record	New York City
Pacific Caterer	Seattle, Wash.
Pacific Coast Record	Los Angeles, Calif.

Pacific Northwest Hotel News	Portland, Ore.
Plant-Restaurant Management	Chicago, Ill.
School and College Cafeteria	Chicago, Ill.
Southern Hotel and Restaurant News	New Orleans, La.
Southern Hotel Reporter	New Orleans, La.
Steward, The	New York City
Tavern Talk	Kansas City, Mo.
Texas Hotel News	San Antonio, Tex.
Western Hotel Reporter	San Francisco, Calif.
Wisconsin Hotelman	Milwaukee, Wis.

HOUSE FURNISHING GOODS

House Furnishing Journal	Chicago, Ill.
House Furnishing Review	New York City

ICE AND REFRIGERATION

A. S. R. E. Journal	New York City
Ice and Refrigeration	Chicago, Ill.
Ice Industry	New York City
Refrigerating Age	San Francisco, Calif.
Refrigerating World	New York City
Refrigeration	Atlanta, Ga.

INDUSTRIAL

Dodge Idea	Mishawaka, Ind.
Employer	Oklahoma City, Okla.
Factory	Chicago, Ill.
Industrial Index	Columbus, Ga.
Industrial Management	New York City
Pictorial Edition of Above	New York City
Industrial Power	Chicago, Ill.

Industrial Survey	Cleveland, Ohio
Invention and Manufacturing	Washington, D. C.
Management Engineering	New York City
Manufacturer, The	Salem, Ore.
Manufacturers' News	Chicago, Ill.
Manufacturers' Record	Baltimore, Md.
100%, The Efficient Magazine	Chicago, Ill.
Pacific Factory Developer	San Francisco, Calif.

JEWELRY, WATCHMAKING, OPTICAL, ETC.

American Jeweler	Chicago, Ill.
Jewelers' Circular	New York City
Keystone, The	Philadelphia, Pa.
Keystone Magazine of Optometry	Philadelphia, Pa.
Manufacturing Jeweler	Providence, R. I.
Mid Continent Jeweler	Kansas City, Mo.
National Jeweler	Chicago, Ill.
Northwestern Jeweler	Albert Lea, Minn.
Optical Journal and Review	New York City
Pacific Goldsmith	San Francisco, Calif.

LAUNDRY

American Laundry Journal	Troy, N. Y.
Laundry Age	New York City
Laundryman's Guide	Atlanta, Ga.
National Laundry Journal	Chicago, Ill.
Pacific Laundry Journal	San Francisco, Calif.
Starchroom Laundry Journal	Cincinnati, Ohio

LUMBER

American Lumberman	Chicago, Ill.
Gulf Coast Lumberman	Houston, Texas
Hardwood Record	Chicago, Ill.
Lumber (Dealer's Edition)	St. Louis, Mo.
Lumber (Manufacturers' Edition)	St. Louis, Mo.
Lumber Trade Journal	New Orleans, La.
Lumber World Review	Chicago, Ill.
Lumberman's Review	New York City
Mississippi Valley Lumberman	Minneapolis, Minn.
New York Lumber Trade Journal	New York City
Retail Lumberman	Kansas City, Mo.
Southern Lumber Journal	Wilmington, N. C.
Southern Lumberman	Nashville, Tenn.
Timberman, The	Portland, Ore.
West Coast Lumberman	Seattle, Wash.

MACHINERY

Abrasive Industry	Cleveland, Ohio
American Machine and Tool Record	Chicago, Ill.
American Machinist	New York City
A. S. M. E. Condensed Catalogues	New York City
Belting and Transmission	Chicago, Ill.
Boiler Maker, The	New York City
Compressed Air Magazine	New York City
Hitchcock's Machine Tool List	Chicago, Ill.
Machinery	New York City
Mac Rae's Blue Book	Chicago, Ill.

Mechanical Engineering	New York City
Mill Supplies	Chicago, Ill.
Pacific Machinery Review	San Francisco, Calif.
Steam	New York City
Western Machinery World	San Francisco, Calif.
Woodworking Machinery List	Chicago, Ill.

MATERIAL HANDLING

Material Handling Cyclopedia	New York City
Material Handling Magazine	Chicago, Ill.

MEDICAL AND SURGICAL

Abstracts of Bacteriology	Baltimore, Md.
Am. Journal of Clinical Medicine	Chicago, Ill.
Am. Jl. of Diseases of Children	Chicago, Ill.
Am. Journal of Medical Science	Philadelphia, Pa.
Am. Jl. of Obstetrics and Gynecology	St. Louis, Mo.
American Journal of Surgery	New York City
American Journal of Syphilis	St. Louis, Mo.
Am. Journal of Tropical Medicine	Baltimore, Md.
American Medicine	New York City
Am. Physician-Medical Council	Philadelphia, Pa.
Annals of Surgery	Philadelphia, Pa.
Archives of Dermatology and Syphilology	Chicago, Ill.
Archives of Internal Medicine	Chicago, Ill.
Archives of Neurology and Psychiatry	Chicago, Ill.
Archives of Pediatrics	New York City
Boston Medical and Surgical Journal	Boston Mass.

California State Jl. of Medicine	San Francisco, Calif.
Chicago Medical Recorder	Chicago, Ill.
Chiropody Record	Chicago, Ill.
Colorado Medicine	Denver, Colo.
Electric Medical Journal	Cincinnati, Ohio
Illinois Medical Journal	Chicago, Ill.
Indianapolis Medical Journal	Indianapolis, Ind.
International Journal of Orthodontia and Oral Surgery	St. Louis, Mo.
International Journal of Surgery	New York City
Journal of Abnormal Psychology	Boston, Mass.
Journal-Lancet	Minneapolis, Minn.
Journal of American Institute of Homeopathy	Chicago, Ill.
Journal of Am. Medical Association	Chicago, Ill.
Journal of Arkansas Medical Society	Little Rock, Ark.
Journal of Bacteriology	Baltimore, Md.
Journal of Cancer Research	Baltimore, Md.
Journal of Comparative Psychology	Baltimore, Md.
Journal of Florida Medical Ass'n.	Jacksonville, Fla.
Journal of Georgia Medical Ass'n.	Atlanta, Ga.
Journal of Immunology	Baltimore, Md.
Journal of Indiana Medical Ass'n.	Fort Wayne, Ind.
Journal of Iowa State Medical Society	Des Moines, Iowa
Journal of Kansas Medical Society	Topeka, Kansas
Journal of Laboratory and Clinical Medicine	St. Louis, Mo.
Journal of Maine Medical Ass'n.	Portland, Me.

Journal of Medical Society of N. J.	Orange, N. J.
Journal of Mich. State Medical Society	Grand Rapids, Mich.
Journal of Mo. State Medical Ass'n.	St. Louis, Mo.
Journal of National Association of Chiropodists	New York City
Journal of Nervous and Mental Disease	New York City
Journal of Oklahoma State Med. Association	Muskogee, Okla.
Journal of Osteopathy	Kirksville, Mo.
Journal of Pharmacology and Experimental Therapeutics	Baltimore, Md.
Journal of S. Carolina Medical Ass'n	Seneca, S. C.
Journal of Tennessee Medical Ass'n.	Nashville, Tenn.
Journal of Urology	Baltimore, Md.
Kentucky Medical Journal	Louisville, Ky.
Larynoscope, The	St. Louis, Mo.
Long Island Medical Journal	Brooklyn, N. Y.
Medical Brief	St. Louis, Mo.
Medical Critic and Guide	New York City
Medical Economist	Brooklyn, N. Y.
Medical Herald and Electro Therapist	Kansas City, Mo.
Medical Life	New York City
Medical Pickwick	New York City
Medical Record	New York City
Medical Record and Annals	San Antonio, Texas
Medical Review of Reviews	New York City
Medical Sentinel	Portland, Ore.

Medical Standard	Chicago, Ill.
Medical Summary	Philadelphia, Pa.
Medical Times	New York City
Medical World	Philadelphia, Pa.
Medicina Clinica	Chicago, Ill.
Military Surgeon	Washington, D. C.
Minnesota Medicine	St. Paul, Minn.
Nation's Health, The	Chicago, Ill.
Nebraska State Medical Journal	Omaha, Neb.
New Orleans Medical and Surgical Journal	New Orleans, La.
New York Medical Journal	New York City
N. Y. State Journal of Medicine	New York City
Northwest Medicine	Seattle, Wash.
Official Bulletin Chicago Med. Soc.	Chicago, Ill.
Official Bull. Wayne Co. Med. Soc.	Chicago, Ill.
Ohio State Medical Journal	Columbus, Ohio
Osteopath, The	Kansas City, Mo.
Pennsylvania Medical Journal	Harrisburg, Pa.
Practical Medicine and Surgery	Austin, Texas
Rhode Island Medical Journal	Providence, R. I.
Southern Clinic	Richmond, Va.
Southern Medicine and Surgery	Charlotte, N. C.
Southern Medical Journal	Birmingham, Ala.
S. W. Journal of Medicine and Surgery	El Reno, Okla.
Southwestern Medicine	El Paso, Texas
Surgery, Gynecology and Obstetrics	Chicago, Ill.

Texas State Journal of Medicine	Forth Worth, Texas
Therapeutic Gazette	Detroit, Mich.
Virginia Medical Monthly	Richmond, Va.
Weekly Roster and Medical Digest	Philadelphia, Pa.
Weekly Bulletin of The St. Louis Medical Society	Chicago, Ill.
West Virginia Medical Journal	Huntington, W. Va.
Western Medical Review	Omaha, Neb.
Western Medical Times	Denver, Colo.
Western Osteopath	Oakland, Calif.
Wisconsin Medical Journal	Milwaukee, Wis.

METAL TRADES

Am. Metal Market and Daily Iron and Steel Report	New York City
Blast Furnace and Steel Plant	Pittsburgh, Pa.
Brass World and Plater's Guide	New York City
Daily Metal Reporter	New York City
Daily Metal Trade	Cleveland, Ohio
Forging and Heat Treating	Pittsburgh, Pa.
Foundry	Cleveland, Ohio
Iron Age, The	New York City
Iron Trade Review	Cleveland, Ohio
Metal Industry, The	New York City
Steel and Metal Digest	New York City
Welding Encyclopedia	Chicago, Ill.
Welding Engineer	Chicago, Ill.

MILITARY

Army and Navy Journal	New York City

MILK AND MILK PRODUCTS

Butter, Cheese and Egg Journal	Milwaukee, Wis.
Chicago Dairy Products	Chicago, Ill.
Creamery Journal, The	Waterloo, Ia.
Creamery and Milk Plant Monthly	Chicago, Ill.
Dairy Market Reporter	Sheboygan Falls, Wis.
Dairy Record	St. Paul, Minn.
Dairyman's Journal	St. Louis, Mo.
Delaware Co. Dairyman	Franklin, N. Y.
Elgin Dairy Report	Elgin, Ill.
Journal of Dairy Science	Baltimore, Md.
Milk Dealer, The	Milwaukee, Wis.
Milk News	Chicago, Ill.
Milk Producer	Milwaukee, Wis.
Milk Reporter, The	Sussex, N. J.
Milk Magazine	Waterloo, Ia.
Nestle's Dairyman	Mohegan Lake, N. Y.
Pacific Dairy Review	San Francisco, Calif.
Western Milk Dealer and Dairyman	Seattle, Wash.

MILLINERY

American Milliner	New York City
Fairchild's Millinery Directory	New York City
Illustrated Milliner	New York City
Milliner, The	Chicago, Ill.
Millinery Trade Review	New York City

MILLING, FLOUR, GRAIN, ETC.

Am. Co-operative Manager	Chicago, Ill.
Am. Elevator and Grain Trade	Chicago, Ill.

American Miller	Chicago, Ill.
Commercial Review	Portland, Ore.
Community Miller	Chicago, Ill.
Co-operative Manager and Farmer	Minneapolis, Minn.
Country Grain Shipper	Minneapolis, Minn.
Dixie Miller	Atlanta, Ga.
Doings in Grain at Milwaukee	Milwaukee, Wis.
Feedingstuffs	New York City
Flour and Feed	Milwaukee, Wis.
Grain Dealers Journal	Chicago, Ill.
Millers' Review, The	Philadelphia, Pa.
Milling and Grain News	St. Louis, Mo.
Modern Miller	Chicago, Ill.
National Miller	Chicago, Ill.
Northwestern Miller	Minneapolis, Minn.
Operative Miller	Chicago, Ill.
Price Current--Grain Reporter	Chicago, Ill.
Rice Journal	Beaumont, Texas
Round-up	Chicago, Ill.
Western Grain Journal	Kansas City, Mo.

MINING

Am. Zinc and Lead Journal	Joplin, Mo.
Arizona Mining Journal	Phoenix, Ariz.
Engineering and Mining Journal	New York City
Mining and Metallurgy	New York City
Mining and Scientific Press	San Francisco, Calif.
Mining Catalog	Pittsburgh, Pa.

Mining Congress Journal	Washington, D. C.
Northwest Mining Truth	Spokane, Wash.
Salt Lake Mining Review	Salt Lake City, Utah
Seilling's Mining Review	Duluth, Minn.
West Virginia Mining News	Charleston, W. Va.

MISCELLANEOUS

American Barber	Atlanta, Ga.
American Hairdresser	Brooklyn, N. Y.
Barber's Journal	New York City
Beauty Culture	New York City
Broom and Broom Corn News	Arcola, Ill.
Brooms, Brushes and Handles	Milwaukee, Wis.
Distribution and Warehousing	New York City
Fishing Gazette	New York City
Glover's Review	Gloversville, N. Y.
Insurance Field	Louisville, Ky.
Insurance Salesman	Indianapolis, Ind.
Journal of The Am. Bar. Ass'n	Chicago, Ill.
Merchants' Records and Show Window	Chicago, Ill.
Nat'l Tent and Awning Mfrs. Review	St. Paul, Minn.
National Underwriter	Chicago, Ill.
Our Mutual Friend	Belton, Texas
Pacific Fisherman	Seattle, Wash.
Purchasing Agent, The	New York City
Raw Material	New York City
Rough Notes	Indianapolis, Ind
Scale Journal	Chicago, Ill.
Sewing Machine Times	New York City

MOTION PICTURES

Amusements	Minneapolis, Minn.
Exhibitors' Herald	Chicago, Ill.
Exhibitors' Trade Review	New York City
It	Los Angeles, Calif.
Moving-Picture Age	Chicago, Ill.
Motion-Picture News	New York City
Moving-Picture World	New York City
Picture-Play News	Rochester, N. Y.
Theatrical Motion-Picture Trade Directory	New York City

MOTOR BOATING

Motor Boat	New York City
Motor Boating	New York City
Open Exhaust	La Crosse, Wis.
Pacific Motor Boat	Seattle, Wash.
Power Boating	Cleveland, Ohio
Rudder, The	New York City
Yachting	New York City

MOTORCYCLE AND BICYCLE

Motorcycle and Bicycle Illustrated	New York City
Motorcycling and Bicycling	Chicago, Ill.
Western Motorcyclist and Bicyclist	Los Angeles, Calif.

MUNICIPAL AND COUNTY GOVERNMENT

American City	New York City
American Municipalities	Marshalltown, Iowa
City Builder	Atlanta, Ga.
County Officials Magazine	Milwaukee, Wis.

Kansas Municipalities	Lawrence, Kansas.
Minnesota Municipalities	Minneapolis, Minn.
Modern City	Baltimore, Md.
Municipal and County Engineering	Indianapolis, Ind.
Municipality	Madison, Wis.
National Municipal Review	New York City
New Jersey Municipalities	Princeton, N. J.
Pacific Municipalities	San Francisco, Calif.
Public Works	New York City
Seattle Municipal News	Seattle, Wash.
Texas Municipalities	Austin, Texas

MUSIC AND MUSIC TRADE

Crescendo, The	Boston, Mass.
Diapason, The	Chicago, Ill.
International Musician	St. Louis, Mo.
Metronome, The	New York City
M. I. S. T.	New York City
Music and Musicians	Seattle, Wash.
Music News	Chicago, Ill.
Music Trade Indicator	Chicago, Ill.
Music Trades	New York City
Music Trade Review	New York City
Musical Advance	New York City
Musical America	New York City
Musical Leader	Chicago, Ill.
Musical Messenger	Cincinnati, Ohio
Musical Monitor	New York City

Musical Observer	New York City
Musicale, The	Dallas, Texas
Musician, The	New York City
New Music Review	New York City
Popular Songs Monthly	Indianapolis, Ind.
Presto	Chicago, Ill.
School Music	Keokuk, Iowa.
Violinist, The	Chicago, Ill.
Violin World	New York City
Western Music Trade Journal	San Francisco, Calif.

NOTIONS; STAPLE AND FANCY GOODS

American Notions	Yonkers, N. Y.
Notion and Novelty Review	New York City

OIL, COTTON SEED

Cotton and Cotton Oil News	Dallas, Texas
Cotton Oil Magazine	Atlanta, Ga.
Oil Mill Gazetteer	Wharton, Texas
Oil Miller, The	Atlanta, Ga.

PAINTING, PAINTS AND DECORATING

Am. Paint and Oil Dealer	St. Louis, Mo.
American Paint Journal	St. Louis, Mo.
Decorating and Painting Contractor	Chicago, Ill.
Drugs, Oils and Paints	Philadelphia, Pa.
Paint, Oil and Chemical Review	Chicago, Ill.
Painter and Decorator	Lafayette, Ind.
Paint and Varnish Record	New York City
Painters' Mag. and Paint and Wall-Paper Dealer	New York City
Western Paint Industry Review	San Francisco, Calif.

PAPER

American Paper Merchant	Chicago, Ill.
Daily Mill Stock Reporter	New York City
Paper	New York City
Paper Industry	Chicago, Ill.
Paper Mill and Wood-Pulp News	New York City
Paper Trade Journal	New York City
United States Paper Maker	New York City

PETROLEUM

California Oil World	Los Angeles, Calif.
Lubrication World	Chicago, Ill.
Mining and Oil Bulletin	Los Angeles, Calif.
National Petroleum News	Cleveland, Ohio
Oil Age	Los Angeles, Calif.
Oil City Derrick	Oil City, Pa.
Oildom	New York City
Oil and Gas Journal	Tulsa, Okla.
Oil and Gas Man's Magazine	Butler, Pa.
Oil and Gas News	Kansas City, Mo.
Oil Field Engineering	Cincinnati, Ohio
Oil News	Galesburg, Ill.
Oil Trade Journal	New York City
Oil Weekly, The	Houston, Texas
Oil World, The	Shreveport, La.
Petroleum Age	Chicago, Ill.
Petroleum Journal	Wichita, Kansas
Petroleum Magazine	Chicago, Ill.
Petroleum Record	Los Angeles, Calif.

Petroleum World	Los Angeles, Calif.
Petroleum Year Book	Los Angeles, Calif.
Powell's Oil and Gas Directory	Bartlesville, Okla.
Scientific Lubrication and Liquid Fuel	Chicago, Ill.
Southwestern Oil Journal	Fort Worth, Texas
Texas Oil Gazette	Fort Worth, Texas
Texas Oil Ledger	Fort Worth, Texas
Wyoming Oil World	Casper, Wyo.

PHOTOGRAPHIC

Abel's Photographic Weekly	Cleveland, Ohio
American Photography	Boston, Mas.
Bulletin of Photography	Philadelphia, Pa.
Camera, The	Philadelphia, Pa.
Camera Craft	San Francisco, Calif.
Photo-Era Magazine	Wolfeboro, N. H.
Photographic Journal of America	Philadelphia, Pa.

PLUMBING, HEATING AND VENTILATING

Domestic Engineering	Chicago, Ill.
Heating and Ventilating Magazine	New York City
Journal Am. Soc'y Heating and Ventilating Engineers	New York City
Merchant Plumber and Fitter	New York City
Plumber and Steam Fitter	New York City
Plumbers' Trade Journal, Steam and Hot Water Fitters' Review	New York City
Warm Air Heating and Sheet Metal Journal	Philadelphia, Pa.
Western Plumber	San Francisco, Calif.

POTTERY AND GLASS

China, Glass and Lamps	Pittsburgh, Pa.
Glass Industry, The	New York City
Glassworker, The	Pittsburgh, Pa.
Keramic Studio	Syracuse, N. Y.
National Glass Budget	Pittsburgh, Pa.
Pottery Glass and Brass Salesman	New York City

POWER PLANTS

International Steam Engineer	Chicago, Ill.
National Engineer	Chicago, Ill.
Power	New York City
Power Plant Engineering	Chicago, Ill.
Southern Engineer	Atlanta, Ga.
Universal Engineer	New York City

PRINTING AND TYPOGRAPHY

American Pressman	Pressmen's Home, Tenn.
American Printer	New York City
Ben Franklin Monthly	Chicago, Ill.
Buckeye County Printer	Somerset, Ohio
Inland Printer	Chicago, Ill.
National Lithographer	New York City
National Printer-Journalist	Chicago, Ill.
Pacific Printer and Publisher	San Francisco, Calif.
Printing	New York City
Printing Art	Cambridge, Mass.
Scott's Printer and Publisher	Lincoln, Neb.
Typographical Journal	Indianapolis, Ind.

RAILROAD

Aera	New York City
Car Builders' Dictionary and Cyclopedia	New York City
Electric Railway Journal	New York City
Electric Traction	Chicago, Ill.
Locomotive Dictionary and Cyclopedia	New York City
Maintenance of Way Cyclopedia	New York City
Official Railway Guide of Chicago	Chicago, Ill.
Pocket List of Railroad Officials	New York City
Railroad Herald	Atlanta, Ga.
Railway Age	New York City
Railway and Locomotive Engineering	New York City
Railway and Marine News	Seattle, Wash.
Railway Electrical Engineer	New York City
Railway Journal	Chicago, Ill.
Railway Maintenance Engineer	Chicago, Ill.
Railway Mechanical Engineer	New York City
Railway Purchases and Stores	Chicago, Ill.
Railway Review	Chicago, Ill.
Railway Signal Engineer	Chicago, Ill.
Traffic Bulletin	Chicago, Ill.
Watts Official Railway Guide	Atlanta, Ga.

REAL ESTATE

National Real-Estate Journal	Chicago, Ill.
N. J. Comm. and Finance Record and Guide	Newark, N. J.
Record and Guide	New York City
Record and Guide	Providence, R. I.

RUBBER TRADE

India Rubber Review	Akron, Ohio
India Rubber World	New York City
Rubber	Cleveland, Ohio
Rubber Age, The	New York City

SEEDS AND NURSERY TRADE

American Nurseryman	Rochester, N. Y.
American Seedsman	Chicago, Ill.
National Nurseryman	Hatboro, Pa.
Seed World	Chicago, Ill.
Seed Trade Buyers' Guide	Chicago, Ill.

SHEET METAL WORKING

Sheet Metal Worker	New York City

SHIPPING, MARINE AND WATERWAYS

American Marine Engineer	Washington, D. C.
Funnel, The	New York City
Gulf Marine Register	New Orleans, La.
Marine Engineering	New York City
Marine Journal	New York City
Marine News	New York City
Marine Review	Cleveland, Ohio
Motorship	New York City
National Marine	New York City
Nautical Gazette	New York City
Nauticus	New York City
Pacific Marine Review	San Francisco, Calif.
Port and Terminal	New York City
Sea Power	Washington, D. C.

Shipbuilding Cyclopedia	New York City
Shipping	New York City
Southern Marine Journal	Houston, Texas
Sterling Marine Catalog	New York City

SHOE AND LEATHER

Am. Shoe and Leather Exporter	Boston, Mass.
American Shoemaking	Boston, Mass.
Boot and Shoe Recorder	Boston, Mass.
Coast Shoe Reporter	San Francisco, Calif.
Finder's Customer	Boston, Mass.
Finder's Salesman	Boston, Mass.
Hide and Leather	Chicago, Ill.
Leather Manufacturer, The	Boston, Mass.
Shoe Findings	Boston, Mass.
Shoe and Leather Facts	Philadelphia, Pa.
Shoe and Leather Reporter	Boston, Mass.
El Reporter Latino Americano	Boston, Mass.
Shoe Repair Shop	Chicago, Ill.
Shoe Repair and Dealer	Boston, Mass.
Shoe Retailer	Boston, Mass.
Shoe Topics	Boston, Mass.

SOAP AND PERFUMERY

Am. Perfumers and Essential Oil Rev.	New York City
Perfumer's Journal Essential Oil Recorder	New York City
Toilet Requisites	New York City

SPORTS AND SPORTING GOODS

Billiards Magazine	Chicago, Ill.
Course and Club House	New York City
Sporting Goods Dealer, The	St. Louis, Mo.
Sporting Goods Gazette	Syracuse, N. Y.
Sporting Goods Journal	Chicago, Ill.
Western Sporting Goods Review	San Francisco, Calif.

STATIONERY AND OFFICE EQUIPMENT

Am. Stationer and Office Outfitter	New York City
Bookseller and Stationery	New York City
Crowley's Magazine	New York City
Geyer's Stationer	New York City
Modern Stationer and Bookseller	New York City
Office Appliances	Chicago, Ill.
Pacific Stationer	San Francisco, Calif.
Typewriter Topics	New York City
Walden's Stationer and Printer	New York City

STONE AND ROCK PRODUCTS

American Stone Trade	Chicago, Ill.
Pit and Quarry	Chicago, Ill.
Rock Products	Chicago, Ill.
Stone	New York City

SUGAR AND SUGAR BEET

Facts About Sugar	New York City
Louisiana Planter and Sugar Mfgr.	New Orleans, La.
El Mundo Azucarero	New Orleans, La.
Sugar	New York City
Weekly Statistical Sugar Journal	New York City

TALKING MACHINE TRADE

Phonographs and Talking Machine Weekly	New York City
Talking Machine and Phonograph Record	Chicago, Ill.
Talking Machine Journal	New York City
Talking Machine World	New York City

TAXICAB AND MOTORBUS

National Taxicab and Motorbus Journal	Chicago, Ill.

TELEPHONE AND TELEGRAPH

Bell Telephone News	Chicago, Ill.
Telegraph and Telephone Age	New York City
Telephone Engineer	Chicago, Ill.
Telephony	Chicago, Ill.
Transmitter	Fort Worth, Texas
Wireless Age	New York City

TEXTILE MANUFACTURE

American Silk Journal	New York City
Am. Wool and Cotton Reporter	Boston, Mass.
Cotton	Atlanta, Ga.
Cotton News	Orangeburg, S. C.
Fibre and Fabric	Boston, Mass.
Mill News	Charlotte, N. C.
Silk	New York City
Southern Textile Bulletin	Charlotte, N. C.
Textile American	Boston, Mass.
Textile Colorist	Philadelphia, Pa.
Textile Digest	Philadelphia, Pa.

Textile Manufacturer	Charlotte, N. C.
Textile World	New York City
Textiles	New York City

TOBACCO

Cigar and Tobacco Journal	Minneapolis, Minn.
Retail Tobacconist	Long Island City, N. Y.
Smoke	Seattle, Wash.
Southern Tobacco Journal	Winton-Salem, N. C.
Tobacco	New York City
Tobacco Leaf	New York City
Tobacco Record	Brooklyn, N. Y.
Tobacco World	Philadelphia, Pa.
U. S. Tobacco Journal	New York City
Western Tobacconist	San Francisco, Calif.
Western Tobacco Journal	Cincinnati, Ohio

TOYS AND NOVELTIES

Gift and Art Shop	New York City
Novelty News	Waukegan, Ill.
Playthings	New York City
Toys and Novelties	Chicago, Ill.

TRAFFIC AND TRANSPORTATION

International Trade and Shipping Digest	San Francisco, Calif.
Shipper's Guide	Chicago, Ill.
Traffic World, The	Chicago, Ill.
Transportation	New York City
Transportation World	New York City

TRUNKS, LEATHER GOODS, ETC.

Trunks, Leather Goods and Umbrellas	Philadelphia, Pa.

UNDERTAKERS

American Funeral Director	Grand Rapids, Mich.
Casket, The	New York City
Embalmers' Monthly	Chicago, Ill.
Pacific Coast Undertaker	San Francisco, Calif.
Southern Funeral Director	Atlanta, Ga.
Sunnyside, The	New York City

VETERINARY

Journal of American Veterinary Medical Association	Baton Rouge, La.
Veterinary Medicine	Chicago, Ill.

WASTE MATERIALS (JUNK)

Waste Trade Journal	New York City

WOODWORKING

Veneers	Indianapolis, Ind.
Wood Turning	Milwaukee, Wis.
Wood-Worker, The	Indianapolis, Ind.

WOOL

American Sheep Breeder	Chicago, Ill.
National Wool Grower	Salt Lake City, Utah.

In certain branches of trade are skilled artisans who might with profit market their knowledge in another field. For example, the chef of a large hotel or restaurant could write for several women's magazines, such as "Good Housekeeping," "Woman's Home Companion," "Today's Housewife," "Ladies' Home Journal," information concerning menus for dinners, luncheons, etc., recipes for preparing meats, vegetables or pastries in novel or appetizing ways.

A man or woman holding a position as designer for a woman's clothing manufacturer could correspond with the trade papers covering his industry and also with the foregoing woman's magazines. You might be employed by a concern which manufactures art pottery or cut glass, or which builds period furniture. Magazines such as "House Beautiful" are interested in obtaining new material of this kind for their columns. Photographs are, of course, necessary in such instances. Landscape artists and tree surgeons as well as persons employed under them; architects and students of architecture, and builders may write for "House and Garden," "The Country Gentleman," and "Keith's Magazine," while those interested in mechanical pursuits might find a market for their knowledge in "Popular Mechanics," "Scientific American," "Popular Science Monthly," etc.

While most trade papers instruct correspondents in regard to their rules, dates for closing of forms, etc., some may take it for granted that you know these things. Therefore, make special request for rules and closing dates if they are not sent you on acceptance of your application. Keep a copy of each article sent to a trade paper or magazine until you have been paid for the work; also, make a scrap book of clippings of your articles, since you may some day wish to refer to them.

www.ingramcontent.com/pod-product-compliance
Ingram Content Group UK Ltd.
Pitfield, Milton Keynes, MK11 3LW, UK
UKHW020646140825
7394UKWH00035B/595

9 781023 852838